Rental Property Investing

*Complete Beginner's Guide on How to Create Wealth,
Passive Income and Financial Freedom with
Apartments and Multifamily Real Estate Investing
Even with No Money Down*

By: James Connor

Table of Contents

Introduction

I want to thank you for purchasing this book, *Rental Property Investing - Complete Beginner's Guide on How to Create Massive Wealth, Passive Income and Financial Freedom with Apartments and Multifamily Real Estate Investing Even with No Money Down.*

Are you interested in increasing your wealth by investing in rental properties, but you aren't certain where to begin? Do you think that rental property investing is a good idea for you? Do you want to invest without having to worry about any expensive mortgages or down payments? If yes, then this is the perfect book for you. This book is a beginner's guide to learning about rental property investing. If you are a first-time investor, then I am quite certain that you have plenty of questions. Well, in today's tech-dominated world, a simple Google search can provide you with plenty of information. However, the wealth of information available online can be quite scary, especially for a beginner. That's where this book comes in. Don't worry, because this book will become your go-to guide to learning about rental property investing.

In this book, you will learn everything there is to know about rental property investing. You will learn if rental property investing is a good option for you, the steps to buying your first property, different things you must consider while buying a rental property, how to analyze the property, raising funds to buy your first rental property, how to manage the property, and much more. Rental property investing is a great way to generate additional income or even passive income. Regardless of your reason for investing, you must understand all the different aspects involved in investing if you want to be profitable.

So, if you are ready to step into the world of rental property investing, let us get started without further ado!

Chapter 1: Rental Property

101

Rental property investing is a great idea - however, how can you determine whether it is the right idea for you or not? As with any other form of investment, there are certain pros and cons involved in rental properties. To begin with, let's talk about the benefits and the possible drawbacks of rental property investing.

Pros and Cons of Rental Property Investing

Direct income

The most obvious benefit of investing in rental properties is that you will be receiving income from your renters. It is a direct source of income. The monthly checks you receive will go directly to your monthly income. For instance, if you decide to rent a property for about $1000 a month, that's $12,000 in the form of additional income per year. Even if this number sounds rather optimistic to you, you stand to gain at least 75% of this from rents. It certainly is a good source of additional income. Apart from this, it is a great source of passive income. Once you rent your property, you don't have to do anything other than collect rents and ensure the property is well maintained. You don't have to quit your day job to become a rental property investor. If you want to, you can always hire a property manager to take care of the property. By doing this, you can drastically reduce the efforts involved in managing the property and can collect your rent checks with no hassle on your end.

Appreciation of the property

Since you happen to own the property, you will stand to gain when the property's value appreciates. Over time, the value of the property does appreciate. So, if you do want to sell in the future, you can expect a profit from the sale.

Sweat equity

Whenever you upgrade the property or make any improvements to it, it increases the sweat equity of the property. If you repaint, get some landscaping done or refurbish it, the property's value will increase. Whenever the value of the property increases, the rent you can demand for the property increases, too. All of this means that it will increase your income.

Tax benefits

There are a couple of tax deductions you can claim as a property owner. All the deductions will help reduce your taxes and increase your earnings. For instance, one of the most considerable deductions available to the owner of a rental property is the interest paid toward the mortgage or any other loan. Any interest payable on a loan that is taken to acquire or improve the property is a deductible expense. The deduction of real estate depreciation is another tax concession available. Also, the cost of any ordinary and necessary repairs of a reasonable amount is deductible, too, like the costs incurred to fix the floor, gutters or any leaks, replacement of a broken window, and more. If you decide to use any of your personal property to further a rental activity, then such property is applicable to tax deductions. Any insurance premiums you pay for the rental property along with any professional or legal services you hire for the maintenance of the rental property are eligible for tax concessions. All in all, these deductions help reduce your tax liability.

As with any other investment, there are certain drawbacks of investing in a rental property, and they are as follows.

If you decide to invest in a rental property, then you must be prepared to allocate a significant share of your assets toward this investment. At least, that's is the case for an average investor. The problem crops up when there is no diversification of your assets. All investors hope to gain profits from their potential investments. However, if it doesn't go as planned and the returns you earn aren't favorable, then you can incur a loss. But don't you fret, because in this book you will learn about different things you can do to ensure your rental property proves to be a profitable investment.

Finding a good tenant is quite important. If you end up with a troublesome tenant, you might find yourself in a sticky situation. What will you do if the tenant doesn't pay rent on time or damages the property? Finding a good tenant is quintessential.

Once you rent out a property, your work doesn't end there. You don't have to be involved in maintaining the property at all times, but you do need to show some involvement. No stream of income is 100% passive, and the same stands true for rental property investing, too. There are certain expenses you need to cover while renting out a property. You can certainly deduct some expenses, but there are limits established for every deductible expense, and anything above that limit is payable by you.

So, there are certain drawbacks, but when it comes to rental property investing, the benefits it offers easily outweigh the drawbacks. A little effort and due diligence can help overcome those drawbacks, too.

Identify Your Investment Goals

Now that you are aware of all the different benefits you stand to gain from investing in rental property, you must identify your investment goals. Why do you want to invest? Failure to plan is translated into planning to fail. It is quintessential to have a sense of purpose, regardless of what you want to do. So, what's the purpose of investing? The reasons for investing will vary from one person to another. Without a plan, it is unlikely that the odds will be in your favor. Without a goal and a plan to achieve that goal, the investment you plan to make will not do you much good. Why do you need a goal? A goal helps motivate you even when obstacles crop up. Only when you consider your goal will you be able to estimate your budget and the associated risks and returns you want.

So, before you can start investing, it is time to think about your investment goals. Do you wish to save for your retirement? Do you want to create a fund for a rainy day? Do you want to create an additional source of income? Does the idea of passive income appeal to you? Do you want to save for your child's education or some other reason? The reasons for investing are quite varied, and you must understand your motivation to invest.

Take some time and think about the different reasons you want to invest. Once you are aware of the reasons, it is time to classify them. Categorize your goals as short-term and long-term goals. A short-term goal might be to save for an exotic vacation, whereas a long-term goal would be to save for your retirement and so on. You get the idea, right? Don't make a mental list of your goals. Instead, make a physical note of the goals. It is always a good idea to write them down. When you make a list of your goals and glance at it regularly, it will act as a motivating factor.

Once you are aware of your goals, you need to make them money specific. The goal "I want to save for an exotic vacation" is quite vague. It neither includes a time limit nor a monetary value. So, the next step is to attach a monetary value to your goals. For instance, if you want to save for a trip to Italy for a week, you need around $15,000 for it. Try to set a monetary value so that you know how much you need to earn to attain that goal.

Principles of Success

Who doesn't desire or dream about success? Everyone does, but only a few tend to be successful.

Did you ever wonder why this happens? If real estate investing is profitable, then why aren't all real estate investors successful? Well, there are certain habits that all successful people share. In this section, you will learn about the five principles for succeeding as a rental property investor.

Learn to manage efficiently

Regardless of whether you are a newbie or a veteran investor, the first key element of becoming a successful rental property investor is to become a good manager. You might have a property manager, or you might want to self-manage, but regardless of which you choose, you still need to be a good manager. Being an owner of rental property is like learning to walk a tightrope. You need to keep moving on that narrow line, and even when a gust of wind threatens to blow you over, you must maintain your balance and keep going. The metaphorical "gust of wind" in the world of rental property investing can come in different forms. It can be in the form of natural disasters, untrustworthy property managers, bad tenants, poor economic conditions, and so on. These things can easily make you falter if you aren't careful. Don't assume that by merely purchasing a property and renting it out, your work ends. Apart from managing the properties, you need to manage your finances. Ensure that you are keeping track of all your expenses in an orderly fashion along with the income you are earning if you want to become a successful investor.

Increasing your income

As you make your way through investing, one of your goals must be to increase your income from rental properties. I am not implying that you need to keep increasing the rent, even if it is an important means of increasing your rental income. You must ensure that the property you rent is never less than the market rate. Now, you might be thinking that renting the property at a price less than the market rate might spell less drama. It might be true, but what is the opportunity cost involved?

Please keep in mind that becoming a rental property investor is like starting a business. Profit needs to be one of your goals if you want to be successful. The more rental units you own, the more problematic it becomes if you rent them out below the market rate. For instance, if you have five units and you rent them out at $100 less than the market rate, then you stand to lose $500 per month and $6000 per year. Now, I am not saying that you need to price the property too high. If you over or under price the rent of the property, then you stand to lose and not gain.

If you want to invest in a property, you must be aware of all the numbers involved. This means it is time to crunch some numbers. You must do the necessary research about the prevailing market rate in the immediate locality. You must also be aware of all the expenses involved.

Reduce the expenses

You will need to work on reducing your expenses. You don't have to become a miserly landlord, but you need to cut costs while making sure that your tenants stay happy. For instance, you can opt for energy-saving appliances in the rental unit. You can transfer the payment of utility bills like water, garbage, and electricity over to the tenant. Compare the insurance policies available to get the best possible rates and the like. These are simple ways in which you can reduce the expenses involved. At times, even a small change can help improve your bottom line.

The property matters

The location of the property is one of the most important aspects of rental property investing. For instance, if you decide to invest in a rental property that is located in an area with poor connectivity, then it is unlikely that you will find a tenant and even if you do, they might not agree to pay a high rent. The location of the property dictates the amount you can quote as rent. Likewise, if you decide to invest in an extremely noisy and polluted industrial area, the demand for the property might not be too high.

Tenants

It isn't merely about finding an ideal property to invest in; you must also find suitable tenants. You must screen all potential tenants while renting out a property. Regardless of how wonderful the property is, without the right tenants, you will not profit. You must ensure you are aware of who your tenants are, their rental record, as well as obtain any past references or records that provide details about them. You must also perform a background check to ensure the potential tenants can pay the rent.

Investing Strategies

Well, you have a rented property, and you might have a few questions. What's next? What is your exit strategy? How can you make money? Some real estate investors buy rental property to repair and then turn it over. Some tend to buy them and hold onto them so they have an excellent source of passive income, while others buy them to sell them later when they need money. Which is the best way? Well, the answer is that there isn't a perfect answer to this question. The key is to know the type of investor you want to be. Here are some options that you can consider.

If you want to hold onto the property for five years or less, you have to flip it. In the early 2000s, house flipping was all the rage. House flipping is still a good strategy today. It requires more patience. Usually, a flipper will purchase the real estate, upgrade it, and then sell it after a couple of months. This investment strategy usually appeals to a conservative or a part-time investor who likes the idea of flipping and tends to have a five-year plan ready. They usually like to take things slowly and then make improvements to the property, rent it out, and then finally sell the property when the market is ripe.

You do not have to sell rentals, even if the real estate market is currently hot. As long as you have stable cash flow, you do not have to sell the property, and this can be a good source of passive income for you. You can keep writing off depreciation on the property for tax purposes until you reach a certain limit. Investors tend to hold onto the property until they can write off the depreciation, and when they cannot, they sell the property.

The third strategy is to keep the property and know that you will sell it when an event occurs that causes a sale. You may plan to sell the property when your child is in college, or for other expenses that you know will be incurred in the future. Some people manage to sell real estate before major repairs such as a new roof are required. However, you may have to sell it at a lower price if you sell a home that requires major repairs. You can, however, use it in the meantime by borrowing it.

If you lose money on a property, you probably want to get rid of it by selling it. Maybe the market has changed and you cannot rent it, maybe insurance or even taxes have soared and you cannot make a profit if you can sell it. There are many things that you need to consider to weigh variables such as the losses that you might incur each month and the scope of any favorable changes before you decide to get rid of the property.

As you have noticed, there is no right answer to this question. Nobody can tell you how long you have to keep the rental property. If you have a plan, stick to it and do not be deterred by market fluctuations.

Type of Investment

If you now want to buy a rental property, you have to choose the type of property you want to buy. There are three main types of real estate to choose from, and they are single-units, multi-unit residential units, and commercial properties.

Single-family units

The best option for an investor who has never rented property before is a single residential property.

They are often cheaper and do not require much maintenance compared to other options. You can invest easily in a single-family unit. It has no common walls, and it is built in a plot by itself. They usually have a front or back yard. Since you are the owner, you are responsible for all maintenance costs incurred on the unit. They tend to attract long-term tenants who are financially sustainable. The resale value of such units is also quite high. The next option is to buy an apartment or a condominium. These are individual units which are part of a large complex or community with common walls. It offers a variety of amenities, including a gym, a club, and a pool. Since you are the owner of the apartment, you are part of a homeowner or a condominium community and have to pay a monthly fee. Maintenance costs are low compared to residential properties consisting of single units. The third option is a townhouse. A townhouse is a mix of a single-family home and an apartment. They usually have common walls with adjoining houses in the neighborhood.

Multi-residential units

These usually consist of two to six portions or units, which an investor buys as a form of investment. A typical situation is when the owner owns the entire building. The owner can live in an apartment and rent the remaining units. The maintenance costs incurred are slightly higher when compared to other forms of real estate investment. However, since they consist of multiple units, the potential for generating higher cash flow is possible.

Real Estate Investment Team

Real estate agents

Everyone wants to make smart decisions whenever there is an economic strain. While investing in a rental property, every penny you spend counts. Everyone has specific criterion when buying a home. Some people want a large house with a pool, and some prefer a cozy apartment. If you are looking for something specific, it is better to seek advice from a professional real estate agent before investing in real estate. You know the exact features that fit your budget and needs, and they can help you with the documentation and throughout the transactional process. A real estate agent will also keep you informed about any other potential properties you can invest in. Some of the benefits of consulting a real estate agent are as follows:

Real estate agents have the right knowledge about making a good deal. They know the right procedures and formalities required to buy and sell real estate. They can also give you the information you need and suggest the right properties, depending on your needs. They also know about the local, state, national, and international market, so they can help you select the ideal property. All of this is possible only if you opt for a good and knowledgeable real estate agent.

Real estate agents who have been in the market for a long time have reliable contacts - people who can provide them the necessary information. By hiring the services of the real estate agent, it also gives you access to such contacts. Apart from this, it also gives you the chance to develop a better connection in the local market and be aware of the properties that you can buy, sell, or rent. They can also enable you to make a profitable decision for your business. They have professional partnerships and contacts in the market and can provide you with a compiled list of contacts they have worked with before.

We all know how cumbersome documentation work is when a property needs to be sold or bought. Real estate agents have gone through this process many times and can help you avoid paperwork mistakes, saving you time and money in the future. Real estate agents will help you to effectively negotiate prices and terms with the other party on your behalf. This will save you trouble and unnecessary tension. These brokers have exceptional negotiation skills. Real estate agents are very experienced and know the value of the land or property and can be sure that you will pay the right price. They can help you find the perfect solution for your budget.

Property manager

There are certain things that you need to consider while deciding whether you want to use the services of a property manager or not. To determine this, you can create a list that things that you need to do, what you cannot do, along with the tasks you don't want to undertake. By hiring a property manager, you no longer have to deal with the tenant's complaints.

Who doesn't like the idea of earning passive income from renting real estate? However, this also means that you have to deal with all the problems and complaints of the tenants. If you use the services of a property manager, you do not have to worry about it. A real estate manager does all of this for you. Your real estate manager will be responsible for things like the selection of tenants. Your real estate manager will take care of all the time-consuming aspects of finding the right tenants for your property. You don't have to spend your precious time checking up on your rental property. For example, the property manager takes care of checking the tenants, site visits, evictions, and so on.

Take a look at the successful real estate magnates, who have managed to accumulate enormous wealth. Do you think they did it all by themselves? Of course, they would not have been able to achieve all their success if they had personally answered every complaint lodged by the renter or had personally corrected the plumbing work on the individual units. They are successful because they are good at prioritizing the tasks and know what is important and what isn't. By hiring a property manager, you can focus your attention on the important aspects of being a landlord.

A real estate management firm offers all kinds of professional services you may need to maintain your property, and you don't have to worry about solving the problem yourself. You save time, energy, and money. You can also do more and sleep better at night, knowing that your investments are in safe hands. Most real estate investors tend to have certain voluntary restrictions on investing in other markets. This is not necessarily bad, but you should not hold back your business. If you have a good property manager, there is no reason why you should not live in another city if you want. You don't have to go to inspect the property physically. The property manager does it all for you. However, I do suggest that it is wise to supervise the work done by the property manager constantly.

A good real estate manager always has your best interests in mind. Before investing in real estate, you can consult with your real estate manager to see if this is a good investment or not. You can ask them various questions about the area you are interested in, the percentage of vacancies, the trends in the local market, the expected rent for real estate, the cost of buying real estate, examining potential real estate and so on. Your real estate manager is your personal advisor who will help you make the best investment decisions.

Hiring a real estate manager is a really good idea. The services they provide outweigh the cost of their hiring. Be careful when you hire a property manager, as the responsibility for the care of your property lies with them. You want someone who can look after your investments and develop them further. You can also focus on other things that require your attention. You can enjoy a steady stream of passive income without having to worry about the various issues involved in maintaining various projects. If you have a few investments in real estate, a real estate manager will help you a lot.

Chapter 2: Sample Plans

Develop a Business Plan

A wish becomes a goal when it is supported with a plan. If you want to get into the business of rental property investing, then you need a business plan to make your dream more realistic. Why do you need a business plan? Well, it helps create a system and set benchmarks to help you successfully create a stream of passive income. Are you wondering what a business plan looks like? In this section, you will learn about the different steps you must follow to create a rental property business plan.

Before getting started, you must understand what a rental property business means. It refers to a venture wherein an investor purchases and manages one or more properties intending to earn a steady income. These properties can be in the form of single or multiple units, which are rented out in exchange for monthly rent. Getting started with rental property investing is like starting any other business. You must figure out the different financing options, do the necessary research, gather the resources, network, and identify your target audience.

So, are you an owner of a rental property business? Well, renting a house can be considered to be a business. This is quite a controversial topic, and there are two ways to look at it. From the perspective of finance, renting a residential property is a source of passive income. Investors aren't liable to pay self-employment tax when it comes to the income derived from rental property or properties. In this sense, renting out properties is not considered to be a business in the strict sense of the word according to tax liabilities. However, from the standpoint of a career option, a lot of people tend to make a full-time income from this passive source. Renting properties can be considered to be a full-fledged business when you think about it from this perspective.

Here are all the steps you must follow for writing a rental property business plan.

- Setting your goals to earn a passive income.

- Selecting the ideal rental property market.

- Estimating all your expenses and the sources of finance.

- Developing a marketing strategy.

- Managing the rental property by yourself or seek outside help.

Let us look at these steps in detail now.

Step one: Setting your passive income goals

Finding tenants is an important part of rental property investing, but it isn't restricted to just that. It is about setting certain goals for this venture, like the time and energy you can direct toward this passive income opportunity. There are two questions you must answer to establish your passive income goals.

How much time and money can you invest? How much passive income do you wish to earn per month?

Step two: Selecting your market

Selecting your market is almost as important as the amount of capital you are willing to invest or the experience you want to gain. There are different factors which influence this decision. However, here are a couple of questions you can use to determine your ideal market.

- Do you want to invest in a distant market?

- If yes, then how distant a market can you invest in?

- Do you have a team to help you handle the daily affairs, or are you willing to commute?

- What is the average rental rate in the market?

- What is the average market price of the property?

You don't necessarily have to live in the vicinity of the market you wish to invest in. That said, this doesn't mean you don't have to understand the market. Once you answer these questions, you will have an ideal market in your mind.

Step three: Estimating all your expenses and the sources of finance

A major hurdle every rental property investor must overcome is figuring out the finances. If you have an estimate of all the different expenses you stand to incur for acquiring and maintaining the rental property, it will give you some much-needed clarity. Your business plan must answer the following questions:

- How much capital will you need to get started?

- How do you plan on raising the capital you need if you don't have it?

- What will be the cost of repairs involved?

- Are there any recurring monthly expenses you will incur? If yes, then what are the expenses?

After you do this, you must also make the offer.

You like the property you want to buy. What do you do next? The next step is to submit the offer for the property.

The process of making an offer to buy a property may vary from state to state. In some areas, verbal communication is appropriate; in others, written consent is required. For various legal reasons, it is advisable to make a written agreement. It helps to get rid of all the confusion and worries. If you have legal problems, you are safe. Negotiations begin when you meet with an agent. The agent will ask you questions to assess your situation and understand what type of property you need. There will be many phone calls, negotiations, and reviews before you can make an offer.

Make sure you fully understand the bidding process. Ask the agent to explain how this process works and contact your lawyer. It is a good idea to consult a financial adviser before deciding on an investment. Know the price you are willing to pay for the property (maximum and minimum restrictions). Remember that this is a negotiation, so be prepared for some back and forth. Research the property extensively. The property should be at your discretion, and in the end, you will invest a significant portion of your finances. Remember the sales motivation of the seller, the date of the calculation, and all the other information you need. You have to be patient, as this is not a process that you can complete overnight. Some property purchases take longer than others. You can ask your lawyer to sign a contract of sale. If the seller suggests the same thing, make sure your lawyer approves it before deciding to sign anything. After all the documents are in order, you can contact your financier to get the allocation approval.

Step four: Marketing strategies

The first step to creating passive income is to purchase a rental property. After that, at some point, you must make a plan about how you can attract tenants to your property. Having a wonderful property that is fully furnished and equipped will do you no good if your target audience isn't aware of it. So, you need to make a list of ways in which you can reach your potential tenants. The most commonly used strategies include publishing ads on rental websites and social networking sites, in print media, by word of mouth through local realtors, local bulletin boards, and the old-school means of word of mouth publicity.

The marketing channel you opt for will depend on your target market. The more specific your marketing strategies are, the easier it will be for you to plan your marketing expenses.

Step five: Managing the rental property

Managing the rental property is quintessential. It involves the managing of all the different systems you must establish to keep the property in good condition and to keep the cash flow going. It doesn't mean you can hire a property manager and leave it all to them. Even if you hire a property manager, you will still need to supervise them. Here are some questions you must answer to understand how you want to manage the property.

• Do you want to be the landlord and self-manage, or do you want to hire a property manager?

• Who will be responsible for finding and screening the tenants?

• Who will look after the upkeep and maintenance of the property?

• Who will look after the basic maintenance of the property like yard maintenance?

The answers to these questions will essentially depend on your budget and the time you wish to allocate. Once you go through all these steps, you will have a clear business plan in mind for rental property investing. Once you have a plan ready, it becomes quite easy to manage the property and avoid any last-minute surprises.

Chapter 3: How to Find Rental Properties

Different Sources to Consider

There are several ways in which potential investors can find rental properties available for sale. When you use multiple sources, you give yourself a chance to find the best properties to invest in. Here are a couple of ways in which you can find great properties.

Through your network

Finding rental properties through networking is a good idea since it helps you discover properties that people might not usually be aware of. Since not a lot of people know about such properties, you might be able to get a good deal on those properties. There are three ways in which you can find properties via networking, and these are through a personal investor network, through any personal acquaintances, and investment clubs.

A personal investor network refers to the database of investors you might have been collecting over months or years that you have been an investor, or it is the database you must start maintaining from now on. It can include the contacts of other landlords you met who own rental properties in the same area as you or anyone else who is an investor and you are well-versed with. Investment clubs are a great way to create useful contacts because they often have an email list wherein members tend to share and advertise real estate properties. If you aren't a member of an investment club, then it is a good idea to become a member now. Most real estate investment clubs tend to charge an annual membership fee of around $100 to $300. Think of this fee as an investment because you stand a chance to gain a lot of valuable information. Your personal network of acquaintances is a great place to start, too. You must remember that those involved in real estate aren't the only ones who can give you access to good investments. Your personal network can include your friends, family members, colleagues, lawyers, accountants, or anyone else along these lines, and they can be great sources of help while you're searching for investment properties. Those who are a part of your personal network might have come across, seen, or heard about some properties that might interest you. Also, if you know any contractors, even they can be an ideal source to network with other landlords or investors.

Find properties online

There are various websites you can use to search for any potential rental property investments. These sites usually offer several resources ranging from a general sale to more refined searches like short sales or foreclosure properties. Some websites even offer information about neighborhoods along with property records that you can analyze to gauge whether the property is a good investment or not.

Realtors can be helpful

There are a couple of different ways in which you can use realtors while searching for rental properties. For instance, if you come across any interesting listings, you can always contact the realtor to arrange a viewing of the property, or you can even view the listings online on their websites. You can contact real estate offices or other realtors who work in the areas you are interested in and inquire about any potential investment properties. You can also enlist the help of a realtor to help you search for potential properties. Realtors tend to have lists of all available properties or have contacts, which might help you.

Don't overlook the print media

You can always find local listings in print media. It might sound a little old-fashioned, but this approach works, too. Some of the properties advertised in print media might not be listed online, so the competition for such properties isn't too high. One of the best sources to find local listings is the newspaper. You can find several "for sale by owner" properties along with properties listed by realtors in your local newspaper. Apart from this, you can also search for rental properties in any local marketing publications. You can find such publications in your local grocery stores and such.

Auctions

Property auctions are also a great way to find good real estate deals. There are different types of auctions you can attend, like online auctions, private auctions, and sheriff sale auctions. A quick Google search can help you find any online auctions for properties in the areas you are interested in. You can also use a site like auction.com to find online auctions. A sheriff sale auction will usually be held in the county's town hall, courthouse, or even the sheriff's office. Usually, foreclosed properties are sold to the public in these auctions. If a specific foreclosed property has not been sold, then the same will be listed as an REO or real estate owned with a local real estate agent. The final option is to look at private auctions held by companies. These auctions are usually contracted by lenders for selling multiple properties at once.

Steps for Choosing an Investment Property

If you have been considered investing in a real estate property, then there are certain steps you must follow while choosing the right property to maximize your investment.

The first thing you must do is talk to others. This means you must first get a feel of the market you want to invest in by talking to other real estate investors in that area. You can attend a meeting of any real estate association in the immediate vicinity to understand the market. Not just that, but as mentioned earlier, networking is one of the best ways to find real estate properties for investing in.

Once you do this, you must estimate all the costs you will acquire in the process of investing in a rental property. It is seldom that an average individual has all the necessary capital just lying around. So, if you want to invest, you must get your finances in order and determine the capital you will need to borrow. Before you start getting excited about any listing, you must also be aware of the costs involved. It is better to prepare in advance to avoid any unpleasant surprises like a monthly payment that's higher than what you imagined.

Now, you must take some time and think about who you want to rent the property to and the kind of neighborhood that will appeal to such tenants. You must find a property that easily fits in with the rest of the neighborhood. For instance, it is not a good idea to invest all your hard-earned money into a tiny dingy studio located in a suburban neighborhood. It is certainly easier to find tenants if you invest in a property that's appropriate for your chosen market.

The TV series Fixer Upper is certainly interesting, but I suggest that a newbie investor steer clear of all fixer-uppers. It is okay to work on improving the appearance of the property like fixing the tiles, repainting the house and such, but you must steer clear of all such works that are related to the core structure of the house like electrical and piping works. If the property you are looking for is absolutely perfect, but the monthly payments related to it are quite high, then I suggest you try house hacking. House hacking refers to the practice of residing in the property for at least a year (when you purchase a duplex and live in one portion or buy a single-family home and rent it to roommates), and it helps you earn a little while making the necessary payments. Not just that, it also becomes quite easy to manage and maintain the property.

Once you find a potential property to invest in, you must acquire all the information related to it. The first step is to figure out the income you stand to gain through rents. If the property was previously let out, then you can ask the previous owner about the property's rental history and compare the rates to those of other properties. A quick online search can also help you understand the current rental rates in the area. If not, you can check in with a local real estate office to get a better idea.

Now, you must tally all your expenses. While estimating your expenses, it is always better to overstate the expenses. So, if the rent you can expect per month is $2000, then you can set $1000 toward different expenses you can expect per month. If you need to pay an EMI of $800 per month, then you can expect a cash flow of $200 from the property. There are different expenses you must consider while making these calculations. You need to include the charges for essential utilities like garbage or water, maintenance costs, major expenses in the form of any repairs, fee of the local homeowners association (if there is one), at least set one month's rent aside for a potential "vacancy," and taxes or insurance. You will learn more about calculating the total cash flow from the property in the following chapters.

Appreciation of the rental property

There are two types of appreciation in the property's value, and they are forced and market appreciation. If you purchase a property and make any repairs, then you are essentially increasing the value of the place, and this is known as forced appreciation. If the neighborhood the property is located in improves over time, then the value of the property is bound to increase, too, and this is known as market appreciation. A new investor must not focus on forced appreciation, because it can be difficult to make a cost-benefit analysis of all the repairs.

On the other hand, market appreciation is easier to estimate, and you can do this by using historical market appreciation data. However, please don't purchase a property only because you think its value will appreciate in the future. A new investor must look for properties that will help generate income, regardless of their value of appreciation, and this is exactly what I suggest you do.

Return rate

There are a couple more calculations you are required to perform. You must estimate your cash on cash rate. For instance, if you invested $100,000 purchasing the property, and if you stand to gain $12,000 per year, then the cash on cash return rate is 12%. A good cash-on-cash return is any number that's over 10%. Before you make a purchase, I suggest you analyze at least two dozen property deals to figure out the cash on cash return rate. However, this must not be the only criterion you use to make a purchase. Also check the condition of the property.

Calculate the capitalization rate

The capitalization, or cap rate, is the time it will take to recover your initial investment. If your initial investment was $100,000 and you earn $5000 annually after deducting all expenses, then the cap rate is 5%. This means it will take you 20 years to recover your investment. If your earnings from the property are $10,000 per year, then the cap rate is 10%, and you will take ten years to recover the initial investment. You will learn more about using the cap rate to analyze a property in the following chapters.

1% Rule

As a rule of thumb, I suggest you use the one percent rule while evaluating any rental properties. If the rent you receive before any expenses is at least 1% of the total purchase price, then the property is a good investment. For instance, if you are purchasing a property for $100,000, then the rent you can expect from it must at least be $1000.

Chapter 4: Analyzing a Rental Property

Unlike a stock market investment, ascertaining the exact value of a property you own or wish to purchase is slightly tricky. In this chapter, you will learn about different aspects you must consider while analyzing a rental property's value.

The Big Picture

When you are trying to analyze the value of a property, you must consider certain essential aspects like the ones discussed in this section.

Income matters

When you are investing in rental property, you must be able to ascertain the realistic income you stand to gain from the property and whether it will be sustainable for you. The present and historical data about the rents related to the property matter. Once you are aware of the income range, then you will be able to calculate the gross earnings from the property and compare this against the numbers of other properties in the same area.

Price appreciation

A housing bubble takes place, and then a crash soon follows. This phenomenon occurs because investors tend to forget about the income component of the property and instead solely focus on the property's potential for appreciation. This was the main reason for the most well-known real estate crash. Investors were not interested in the negative cash flow they had to endure and instead concentrated only on the profits they could gain from a flip within a year or two. Once the party came to a standstill, speculators were crushed and this, in turn, caused a domino effect which hurt all those who were in the "buy and hold" stage of the property. If your primary focus is on the appreciation of the property's value in the future instead of the income, then you are a speculator. Real estate holds no true value until it can generate income for the owner.

Property price and inflation

A property's price will appreciate only if the inflation is around +/- 2%. Simply put, if the current rate of inflation is around 3%, then you can expect a national increase in property prices by 1-5%. Over time, the price can fluctuate drastically. However, if you observe the prices of property for over ten years, you will be able to see an obvious correlation. If you have an impression that the prices of property will increase at a steady rate of 10% per year, then I hate to break your bubble. You must only think of the property's appreciation as a secondary factor and not a primary attribute. If the value does increase, it is amazing. If not, then you will at least have cash flowing in.

Property is localized

Don't place too much emphasis on national property statistics. Just because the prices of property are going up in one region doesn't mean the same statistics apply to you as well. Forget about national statistics while analyzing the property's value. Instead, you must stick to local market trends.

Specific Steps to Follow

Calculate the annual gross yield

Consider the realistic existing monthly rate of rent in the market according to comparables and multiply it by 12 to get your gross annual yield from the property. Now, you must divide the gross yield you get by the current market price of the property. For instance, let us assume the market price of the property is $500,000. If the rent is $2000 per month, it gives you $24,000 per year. Now, divide $24,000 by $500,000. It gives you a gross yield of 4.8%. The annual gross yield is a quick way to analyze what you stand to gain from the property given that you are acquiring the property without a loan and don't have any other ongoing expenditures.

Compare the gross rental yield to the risk-free rate

The risk-free rate is defined as the yield of a 10-year US bond. Investors term it as risk-free because it is practically impossible that the US government will default on any of their debt payments. All investment decisions you make require a risk premium that's more than the risk-free rate. Or else, you must ask yourself why you are even risking all your hard-earned money. If the annual gross rental yield of the property is less than the risk-free rate, then you must either negotiate a better deal or search for another property.

Calculate the annual net rent yield

The net rent yield is essentially your net operating income from the property divided by the market value of the property. It is quite easy to calculate the net annual income. You must subtract the expenses like interest on the mortgage, insurance premiums, property taxes, marketing, and maintenance cost of the property and HOA dues from the gross annual income of the property. Simply put, you must calculate the profit you stand to earn.

For instance, let's say the annual rent is $24,000, the HOA dues are $3000, property taxes amount to $4800, the insurance costs $500, the maintenance is about $1000, and the mortgage interest is $10000. This means your total expenses account for $19,700, and your net income from the property is $4300. So, to calculate the net rental yield, you must divide $4300/$500,000. The net rental yield in this situation is 1%. As long as the cash flow from the rental property stays positive, all is well. However, the margin can differ from one person to another.

Compare the net rental yield to the risk-free rate

The net rental yield must at least be equal to or higher than the risk-free rate. You will repay the initial principal over time, and it will increase the net rental yield and spread over the risk-free rate. If all goes as it should, then the rents will increase along with your property's value.

Price to earnings ratio

The price to earnings ratio is the market value of the property divided by the net operating profits from the property. In the above example, the price to earnings ratio is 106 (i.e., $500,000/$4700). So, that means the investor needs 106 years of net profits to make back the initial investment. This doesn't sound too good, but it is only an example. In this example, it is assumed that the owner never pays down the mortgage, and the rent stays constant - both of these situations are highly unlikely. A better way to crunch numbers is to divide the market price of the property by the gross rental income. In the above example, when you follow this formula, it gives you 20.8. It essentially means it will take the property 20.8 years to pay for itself. The lower the price to earnings ratio, the better deal it is.

Property price and rental expectations forecast

The price to earnings ratio along with the rental yield rate are ways to check the income the property will generate, provided everything works favorably. Apart from ratios, you must also concentrate on several external factors while determining whether a specific property is a good investment or not. The best way to forecast what the future holds in store for you is to compare what happened in the past and past real estate development and establish realistic expectations about certain external factors. The external factors that I am referring to are the local employment growth, city permits for development, tax respites, and such. When all these factors are favorable, then the rental price, as well as the value of the property, will increase.

Various situations

Now, you need to establish a realistic property price along with rental forecasts for various scenarios. For instance, if the rental value decreases for the next five years at a rate of 5% per year, will you be able to handle this decrease? If the mortgage rates increase from 3.5% to 5%, how will this influence the demand for real estate? You must be prepared to deal with things if they don't go as you planned. You must develop certain exit strategies to leave the market when things become unfavorable. You will learn more about exit strategies in the following chapters.

Taxes and depreciation

Most of the expenses you incur while maintaining and owning a rental property offer tax deductions, including the interest payable on the mortgage as well as property taxes. Depreciation is a non-cash item that not only decreases your Net Operating Income, but it also reduces your taxes. If you reside in the property for at least two years out of the past five years, then $250,000 and $500,000 of profits are considered to be tax-free for individuals and married couples respectively. There is also a tax provision, the 1031 exchange, which allows an investor to sell a specific property, then reinvest all the proceeds from the sale into a new property while deferring all capital gains taxes.

Cash Flow Analysis

Cash flow refers to the income you are left with from a specific business after you clear all your dues and pay all the necessary bills. In the business of rental property investing, cash flow represents the income you are left with in hand after you pay for different expenses like mortgage, insurance, vacancies, capital expenditure, taxes, utilities, and any other property-related expenses. Cash flow is one of the basic things you need to calculate, and it is quite easy to calculate.

Cash flow = Total income – Total expenditure

It is as simple as that, but a lot of people get it wrong because there are several items you must consider while calculating. If you miss out on even one item, it will affect your cash flow.

Total income

The total income is often the same as the total rent you earn, although at times it might not be. There are a couple of sources of income you must include like application fees, laundry income, and late fees. While analyzing the cash flow from a property, it is a good idea to make a list of all the possible sources of income. While estimating the income you stand to earn, opt for a conservative approach. Essentially, it is a good accounting practice, especially while making estimates, to understate the income and overstate the expenses you might incur. It is a better idea to err on the side of caution and assume you might not get as much as you are hoping to get.

Total expenses

This is the aspect of calculating the slightly tricky cash flow. Most people are good at estimating their income, but when it comes to expenses, making even one mistake can spell the difference between success and failure. While you are dealing with rental properties, there are several expenses you will incur. For instance, here are all the expenses you might incur, just off the top of my head:

The mortgage, property taxes, mortgage insurance, flood insurance, property hazard insurance, earthquake insurance, sewer, garbage, water, repairs, propane, natural gas, electricity, general maintenance, new appliances, landscaping, capital expenditure, software, gas or mileage, office supplies, Homeowners Association dues and fees, city taxes, payroll, property management costs, vacancy rate, advertising, marketing, and a couple of other expenses I might have overlooked.

Apart from making a list of all possible expenses, you must understand that each of these expenses might not be monthly. So, it is a good idea to calculate the specific percentage of those expenses while planning. For instance, your rental property unit might not be vacant right now, but you must function under the assumption that it might be empty at least one month per year. Therefore, while calculating your total expenses, you might want to include vacancy expense as 1/12th of the annual rent. Various expenses like your office supplies or even gas can be ignored while dealing with a single house, but you must consider them if you are dealing with a multi-family rental unit.

Here is an example of how to calculate cash flow to help you understand what each of these items translates into:

Let us take the example of Homer, who is trying to calculate his monthly cash flow from a two-unit family house he wants to buy. According to the local real estate agent, Homer can rent out this property for $600 per unit. He will need to pay $50 for garbage and $125 for water or sewer per month. The real estate agent informs him that the properties like the one he wants to buy tend to stay vacant for 5% of the year. Homer estimates that he will need to spend around 8% per month on all the repairs. Apart from this, he plans on keeping 5% aside every month toward capital expenditures like installation of a new roof, a new heating system, or any other major property-related expenses. Homer has a mortgage on the popery, and his mortgage payment will be around $470 per month without taxes or insurance. The yearly property taxes amount to $960 per year, and the insurance is about $600 per year. Finally, Homer decides to hire the help of a management company, and their charges amount to 10% per month for managing the property.

So, how much cash flow can Homer expect from his property?

Monthly income: $600 x 2 units = $1200.

Monthly expenses: mortgage = $470, insurance= $50, repairs = $96, taxes = $80, vacancy = $60, capital expenditure = $60, water or sewage = $125, garbage = $50 and management expenses = $120. So, the summation of all these expenses gives Homer a monthly expense of $1111 for the rental property.

Cash flow = total income – total expenses

Cash flow, in this case, is $89 per month.

Cash on Cash Return on Investment

If Homer spends $20,000 to acquire the property, what is the cash on cash return on investment for this property? The annual cash flow a rental property investor receives according to the cash that was invested is referred to as the Cash on Cash Return on Investment. This is a simple method that helps the investor figure out the returns from the property when compared with other forms of investment. The formula you must use to calculate the Cash on Cash Return on Investment is:

Cash on Cash Return = Annual cash flow / the total investment

The total cash flow per year is $1068 (monthly cash flow *12), and the initial investment is $20,000. So, the Cash on Cash Return, in this case, is 5.34% ($1068 /$20,000). Please remember that this rate doesn't include any potential appreciation of the rental property, tax benefits, pay down of a loan, or any other items, which can increase or decrease Homer's profit.

Cash Flow using the 50% rule

There is another quick way in which you can estimate the cash flow using a method known as the 50% rule. As a rule of thumb, it is a good idea to assume that 50% of your rental income will go toward expenses without taking into account the mortgage principal or interest payment. The formula is as follows:

Cash flow = (total income x 50%)- mortgage principal and interest

Let us use the information given in the previous section and determine Homer's cash flow using the 50% method. He is expecting to earn $1200 per month as rent, and the mortgage principal and interest payments amount to $470. When you use the 50% rule:

Cash flow = ($1200 x 50%) - $470. So, the cash flow is $130. Keep in mind that this is merely a rule of thumb and is certainly not as accurate as a detailed cash flow statement. In this example, by using the 50% cash flow rule, Homer estimates that he can earn $130 per month, but the detailed cash flow statement shows he can earn only $89 per month. Therefore, it is safe to assume that this method is not fully accurate. However, when you are trying to compare and analyze dozens of properties, using this rule will help you decide whether the property can generate positive cash flow or not. Once you shortlist the properties, you can start crunching the numbers and get a fair estimate instead of a vague one.

Chapter 5: Location of The Property

The location of the property is one of the most important criteria when it comes to rental property investing. By opting for an ideal location, the chances of deriving optimal returns from the property increase. However, if you opt for the wrong location, you might get it at a low price and still incur losses. Real estate tends to be quite local. An investment location that might work for one person might not be the best location for you. Generally speaking, the location you opt for must appeal to your potential renters while being profitable for you. In this section, you will learn about the different steps you can follow while choosing the location of the investment property.

Big-picture Location Criteria

The process of selecting the location of the investment property is similar to using Google Maps. You will start with a zoomed-out view of the entire country or the world. Form the bird's eye view you are presented with, you must consider the major trends which will determine the profitability of the property. Once you do this, you can then judge the property according to different criteria like the neighborhood, connectivity, school district, and more. At this stage, you must consider some major factors like the ones discussed here.

Jobs and economics

A real estate investment will be profitable only if you get the rent you desire and receive it on time. This means you need renters who have good jobs. For instance, if you invest in a rental property in a one-factory town and the factory shuts down, then your investment is bound to suffer. Why does this happen? The vacancies will increase, the rents will decrease, and you will be unable to sell the property for the best market price. So, it is a good idea to study the job market related to the area you want to invest in. Here are certain factors you must consider for determining whether the job market is strong in the area you opted for or not:

• What is the number of jobs present in the overall market? Is this number increasing or decreasing?

• What is the average salary of employees in those areas? Is this number increasing or decreasing?

• What are the types of jobs available in the area? Are the jobs low or high-paying ones?

- Is there any diversification of jobs in the market? Are the usual jobs a source of stable income?

Every location will have its advantages as well as downsides. However, if you notice that the overall job market consists of diversified jobs, has diversification of the types of employees, the average pay seems to be increasing, and the rate of unemployment is low, then it is a good market. You can also obtain information about the same factors discussed above by going through the local newspapers to find out any plans for development in that area.

In the US, if you want to gain information about the job and local economies, then there are a couple of sources you can use like the Chamber of Commerce, BLS.gov, the Comprehensive Annual Financial Report, and the Comprehensive Plan of the city.

Population growth

Another factor that you must consider is population growth. It is intricately related to the jobs and economics of the region. It is normal human behavior to move to those areas that offer better job prospects. However, there are different factors like weather, local politics, housing rates, and natural attractions that contribute to attracting people to a specific location. While thinking about investing in rental properties, you must opt for a region which shows potential for growth in population. When the population increases, the demand for housing tends to increase, too. Remember, if the supply is fixed while the demand increases, then the commodity value increases. So, if there is an increase in demand and the supply of housing properties is limited, then it leads to an increase in the rental value of the property.

Price-rent ratio

The price-rent ratio helps evaluate whether the property has any potential of being profitable or not. You must divide the average housing price prevailing in the area by the average rent. If the price-rent ratio is quite high, then it is usually not a good market to invest in. Ideally, this ratio should be between 5 to 8. However, this is not the only factor you must consider. Also, if the price-rent ratio is quite low in a specific region, maybe it is low for a reason. So, you need to do the necessary research before you come to any conclusions about whether the property is a good investment or not.

Small-scale Location Criteria

Real estate is often a local market, and once you cover all the previous criteria, it is time to zoom into the neighborhood. Here are certain characteristics you must consider while deciding whether a property in a specific neighborhood is a good investment or not.

Convenience

One of the first things you must consider while selecting a property is the convenience it offers. The best way to go about it is to check whether there is a major economic center within ten miles of the property. I know it might sound quite specific, but you must keep this in mind. Now, you might be thinking that it isn't necessary that everyone has to live within a ten-mile radius from their place of employment, shopping centers, or other community centers. Well, take a moment and think about it - if it were possible to live within a ten-mile radius from your place of employment, wouldn't you opt for this instead of living somewhere that's 20 miles away? Most people would prefer this option. You must remember the equation of demand and supply. As an investor, you must give yourself the best chance at becoming an owner of a successful investment where most people would want to live.

Romance

Wait, what has romance got to do with the investment? I am referring to the fuzzy and slightly palpable criteria that attract people to a certain location on an emotional level. After all, selecting a place of residence is often an emotional decision as much as a practical decision. For some places, romance can include the following:

- Streets that are lined with mature trees forming canopies.

- The proximity to parks or any open spaces where people can relax and unwind.

- Quaint coffee shops, restaurants, pubs, and other eateries.

- Picturesque views of mountains, forests, water, or any other scenery.

- The proximity to commercial districts.

The concept of romance is quite subjective, and it will differ from one location to the next. So, it is time to wear your boots and go scout the location for yourself. Now is the time to explore the location for yourself and see what appeals to you. You must make it a point to physically visit the potential locations to see what you like and what will attract your target customers. You must do this even if you are investing in a property in another state.

Crime rates and safety

Regardless of which part of the world you are based in, you will want to live in a safe location with extremely low or no criminal activity. Well, your tenants aren't any different. As a potential landlord, you must understand that crime can cost you money. Imagine the loss you stand to bear if your property is vandalized, if something is stolen, and so on. Not just that, prospective tenants will also be wary of living in an area with a high crime rate. The local crime rate is often difficult to reverse and therefore, I suggest that you stay away from such locations even if the financials look rather appealing on paper. So, how can you obtain the data you need about the crime rates? The first thing you can do is perform a quick online search using different websites like trulia.com maps, spotcrime.com, city-data.com crime reports, or even by performing a simple Google Search. Once you perform the online search, you must go visit the neighborhood. A couple of red flags you must look out for are bars on windows, protective covers for the HVAC units, and even boarded houses. You can talk to the residents of the area, other landlords, and property managers. Apart from this, you can also visit the local police station to inquire about the crime rate in a specific location.

School districts

Since you are interested in investing in rental properties, you must consider the proximity to school districts. It is an important criterion, especially if your target audience includes families. As with the crime rate, a good place to start your research while looking for school districts is the greatschool.com. However, your decision must not be solely based on online research. You must inquire about the same by talking to local real estate agents. They can provide information about the most popular areas according to school districts among the residents. It is all about getting to know the market you want to invest in and the local situation.

Public transport

In an urban area, the proximity to public transportation like buses, trains, and subways is important while selecting the location of the property. If your potential audience uses public transit, then you must concentrate on those areas which offer good public transport connectivity. I suggest you look at maps of the routes that offer connectivity to your chosen location. A simple search on Google Transit can help you find the available public transportation routes around the world. While using such tools, you must also identify the proximity of bus stops and subway stations from the property. Even a 5-minute longer commute can influence the desirability of the property.

Neighborhood covenants

Most of the neighborhoods and apartment complexes tend to have a set of covenants and conditions along with restrictions which dictate what is and isn't acceptable for the residents. While investing in a property, you must consult with a lawyer or an agent to understand all these rules and regulations. The neighborhood covenants, conditions, and restrictions, or the CCRs, are in place to prevent residents from doing things like placing their old and obsolete vehicles in the front yard. On the downside, they can also stop you from renting the property. At times, CCRs also restrict renting out of properties in certain neighborhoods. That is something you must be aware of ahead of time if you want to invest in a rental property!

Apart from the CRRs, some properties also tend to be a part of a local homeowner's association or a condominium association. These associations are non-profit organizations created by the property owners for the enforcement of the CCRs and the maintenance of the common areas. As a prospective homeowner, you will, by default, be a member of the homeowner's association and will need to pay an annual membership fee. The fee can vary from one place to another, so you must inquire about the same since it is a recurring expense on the property. While purchasing a property, you must do thorough research about the CCRs and the homeowner's associations. At this stage, I suggest you steer clear of all properties with excessive fees and extremely restrictive rules which don't provide the necessary value to the homeowner.

Local laws

The laws of local governments - state, county, or city/town - can influence your investment decision. Here are a couple of things you must pay attention to:

The property taxes - are the taxes payable high or low in relation to the rent? Are the local government entities managing their funds properly? Is there a steep and periodic increase in the taxes payable, or are the rates stable? You can refer to the city's comprehensive annual financial report to analyze these factors.

Municipal services - are the property taxes being used to provide necessary municipal services like picking up trash, keeping the streets clean, access to water and drainage, police and fire services, along with the enforcement of the local laws?

Rental license and laws - the local regulation of the rental properties is a trend that's picking up these days. In some areas, the property owners are required to have a rental license, pay an annual fee, and meet the property inspector at the property once every year. These things take up some time and money. Rental laws relate to basic guidelines about the property being equipped with smoke detectors and such. For instance, in some cities, there exists a law which says that if the owner wants to sell the property, then the first right to purchase is given to the tenant.

Rent control - some cities also have certain rent control measures in place that dictate the maximum rent you can charge for a unit or the rent increment you can charge during a specific period. This is something you must pay attention to, since your earnings from the property are subject to rent control laws.

Eviction laws - the government regulates the landlord and tenant laws in the US. Some states tend to be renter-friendly, while the others are landlord-friendly. If you wish to buy a property in a tenant-friendly state, then be prepared for certain extra costs and time you must spend while evicting a bad renter.

You can obtain all this information from the local government's website. Also, you can inquire about the same by calling or visiting a local code enforcement office and asking them about all the relevant laws a potential investor must be aware of.

Barriers to supply

A barrier to supply is one factor that a lot of investors fail to discuss. It is a simple analysis that can help you increase your earnings as an investor. Remember the rule of supply and demand I discussed

61

at the beginning of this chapter? Most of the criteria related to the location of the property tend to affect demand. It means they tend to influence the number of people who might want to rent your property. However, the barriers to supply tend to affect the number of competing units that can be built in the area. The more difficult it is for a new developer to build new units in the area, the greater will be the value of your rental property in such areas. Here are a couple of things you must look for which tend to restrict supply.

- Certain natural borders which prevent any future expansion like lakes, oceans, rivers, or mountains.

- Human made borders that obstruct expansion like protected parks, land, or universities.

- Any rules which restrict the development of land or make construction activity more difficult and expensive.

- Any zoning laws that limit the construction of certain types of properties.

Now that you are aware of the different things you must consider while selecting the location of the property, you must start using the same while determining an ideal location.

Chapter 6: Rental Property Management Strategies

Types of Management Strategies

There are three types of rental property management strategies you can use, and they are as follows.

- Do-it-yourself approach

- Half and half approach

- Outsource the management entirely

The type of management strategy you opt for will depend on the resources available to you - essentially, time and money. Apart from this, your level of experience, as well as the proximity to the rental property, can influence your choice of management strategy. In this chapter, you will learn about these strategies in detail.

Do-It-Yourself Approach

As the name suggests, in this type of management strategy, you will be responsible for everything related to the rental property. You will need to collect the rent, pay the necessary taxes, and take care of all aspects of maintenance of the property.

There are two advantages this method offers. It gives you complete control over your investment property. As a small business owner, having complete control over the operations is a nice advantage. When you take care of all aspects of management, you will become aware of all that's going on in the business. Since you will be taking care of the daily management work, you will be able to detect problems right away. Early detection can help fix the problem quickly and prevent it from recurring.

On the downside, you might not have the necessary knowledge to take care of all aspects of management. No one is an expert at everything. There might be some things you can take care of by yourself and others you might need some help with. For instance, if you hire the services of an accountant instead of doing the taxes by yourself, the accountant might discover certain deductions you weren't aware of. Instead of preparing the rental agreement yourself, if you hire a lawyer to help you with it, the result might be a watertight agreement. Also, hiring professionals will ensure you are getting your money's worth and more. It is always better to hire a handyman to fix any repairs instead of doing them yourself. Since you are wholly and solely responsible for the maintenance and the management of the property, everything rests on your shoulders. It can feel like an overwhelming responsibility to take on, especially for someone who is just getting started. Apart from this, when you try to do everything by yourself, you might make certain mistakes or overlook certain aspects of the business.

This form of management is best suited for landlords who need to look after limited rental units, who have some previous business experience or have managed rental properties in the past, and those landlords who want to have complete control over their property.

Half and Half Approach

While following this method of management, you can manage all those areas that you feel comfortable handling or have the necessary expertise to manage and outsource the rest. This method helps you stay involved in the day-to-day operations while ensuring you get the necessary professional help to take care of all those aspects of management you aren't comfortable handling or don't have the knowledge about.

You can outsource the legal aspects along with the maintenance duties. For instance, you can outsource any issues of rental management related to legal matters. You might be good at managing the finances related to the property, taking care of the daily maintenance work, and managing the complaints, but might not be comfortable while dealing with any legal issues. This can include tasks like drafting a rental agreement which complies with all the necessary laws, or dealing with an eviction process. For such things, it is better to hire a lawyer instead of taking on a responsibility you cannot deal with. You can also outsource the maintenance work, like hiring a handyman or appointing a building superintendent for attending to all the significant maintenance issues while you deal with the other aspects of management.

The benefits of this method are that you will have plenty of time on your hands, since the burden of all the tasks doesn't rest solely on your shoulders. This comes in handy if you want to use the rental property for generating passive income while holding onto your day job. You can use the additional time to do things you like or work on other investment options. Apart from this, you can hire experts to tend to those matters beyond your area of expertise. So, you can ensure that you get the best possible help. The only disadvantage is that you rely on others and must trust that they know what they are doing while they keep your best interest in mind.

This strategy is ideal for all those landlords who own several rental units and are looking to expand their rental units.

Outsourcing Everything

If you are interested in becoming the owner of a rental property but have no desire to manage it, then this is the best option available. By opting for this strategy, you no longer have to worry about being a hands-on manager. If you feel like you are a better investor than manager or if you don't have the time to spend managing the property, then this is a good idea. When you hire a property manager or avail the services of a property management company, then they will take care of all steps of property management like screening the prospective renters, collecting rents, maintenance and repair works, tenant eviction and so on.

The most important advantage of this method of management is that it frees you from the trouble of managing the property. You no longer have to worry about attending to a tenant's complaint about a noisy neighbor at 2 in the morning. Your responsibilities as far as managing the property will be down to the bare minimum. Also, you don't have to worry about finding new tenants or evicting a troublesome renter.

On the downside, this form of management can be rather expensive and will eat into the profits you earn from the rental units. The more units you own, the higher will be the cost of outsourcing. Apart from this, another obvious disadvantage is that you will be placing your business in the hands of others. If the person in charge mismanages the property, then it can cost you dearly. Also, if they don't have your best interest in mind while doing their job, it will do you more harm than good. So, you must ensure that you are thoroughly screening the manager or the management company you wish to hire. You must keep an exit strategy on hand to ensure that you can cut your losses and exit the market when things go bad.

This management strategy is ideal for all those landlords who don't live near the rental property, who have a large number of units to take care of, and those who are looking to diversify their investment portfolio.

Steps of Self-Management

An experienced investor might tell you that managing a rental property by yourself is similar to managing a full-time business. For all those owners who want to earn the rent from the property without having to deal with the tenant's complaints, taking care of the repairs and maintenance work on the property and other related works, then hiring a property manager is the best option available. However, by hiring a property manager, you will be increasing the expenses involved. In spite of all the benefits it offers, a lot of investors don't like the idea of incurring additional costs by hiring a property manager. If you happen to be one of those investors, then the good news is that you can learn to manage the property by yourself. In this section, you will learn about the different steps you must follow if you want to self-manage the rental units without hiring a property manager.

The correct rent

The first step is you must decide the right rent amount for the property. The rent you fix must strike a balance between increasing your income and ensuring the property is always occupied by good tenants. The correct rent can be determined by finding the current rental value in the market or by comparing the rent of other similar properties in the chosen area. When you hire a property manager, this responsibility is transferred to that individual. However, you can do it on your own by doing a little research. There are certain factors which can affect the monthly rent like the number of bedrooms and bathrooms, the different amenities and utilities you provide like gas, internet, or water, whether pets are allowed or not, any additional aspects like a garage facility, additional storage, parking space, and backyard, along with the property's location.

Automate the process

One of the major aspects of managing the property is to ensure that you handle and manage all the tasks in an efficient and timely manner. A lot of real estate investors who are self-managing the rental properties tend to invest in rental properties to create an additional source of income. If you want to self-manage, then be prepared to set some time aside for tasks like property inspection, collection of rent, property maintenance, and the processing of applications. If you can automate certain tedious administrative processes, then you can free up some time for yourself. Various online tools and software like Rentec Direct are designed especially for the management of rental units and help streamline tasks like rent collection, tracking the income and expenses related to the property, screening of tenants, and the marketing works of any vacant units.

Learn the landlord-tenant laws

The laws related to rental housing are established for protecting the interest of landlords as well as tenants. Being aware of all the necessary federal, state, and local laws and compliances is quintessential. Ignorance of the law is not an excuse, and non-compliance with laws can land you in legal trouble. NOLO is a good platform to get started with while researching all the necessary laws and compliances. The US HUD (Department of Housing and Urban Development) governs the regulations related to discrimination and other issues that affect the rights of tenants. You can also check with the local and state real estate boards to learn more about these laws.

Diligent screening

A good tenant will not only take care of the property, but will also pay the rent on time. So, if you wish for smooth sailing as the owner of rental property, then you must concentrate on selecting good tenants. You need to establish a good screening process to ensure you weed out any bad renters and are left with only the good ones. Landlords have certain preemptive rights about renting the property to tenants based on their credit score, rental history, and other factors provided in the rental applications and screening reports. Tenant screening is a very important step, and it helps protect the owner's investment. You will learn more about the screening process in the subsequent chapters.

Legal agreement

It is always better to have a written document instead of relying on a verbal contract. Having a watertight rental agreement is your strongest ally while defining your expectations as well as those of your tenant. A legally binding agreement comes in handy when disputes arise. A good rental contract must clearly outline all the terms and conditions of renting out the property along with the rights and responsibilities of the tenants and the owners. Each state has different laws about the landlord-tenant relationship. So, you must go through those laws while drafting the rental agreement. Make the document as specific as you can and don't make it vague or generic. Also, get the document reviewed by a lawyer to ensure that all the compliances are in order and you aren't contravening any laws.

Property maintenance

Routine and seasonal management of the property, along with regular and emergency maintenance, are important aspects of property maintenance. You must stay on top of it to ensure that your property is protected. As a landlord, you are legally duty bound to ensure that the property is always in habitable condition. It means you must strive to create a safe and habitable condition. It isn't merely about fulfilling your legal obligations, but you must do this to ensure that your tenants are happy. Happy tenants mean less turnover and better rents.

Performing regular inspections

If you want to make sure that your property is being properly maintained, then you must conduct regular inspections. There are two benefits to conducting regular inspections. If there are any maintenance issues, then you will be able to identify them during the inspections and take the necessary action to fix them. It also helps ensure that your tenants are sticking to the rental agreement and are taking reasonable care of the property. If you are self-managing the property, then you must conduct regular inspections, apart from conducting an inspection at the start and termination of the rental agreement.

Insurance is a must

There are insurance policies that are designed for specific needs of a landlord, like protection against any financial loss from the rental property or any other financial obligations related to the rental property. Some owners seem to assume that they can use a regular homeowner's insurance policy to cover the rental unit. However, the coverage offered by such policies is often limited and not sufficient to fully protect your interests. The insurance policy you opt for must cover all the likely liabilities and damages related to rental accommodations.

Tax time

Taxes cannot be overlooked or ignored. By investing in real estate, you will be entitled to certain tax deductions and benefits. You will be allowed to deduct certain expenses like insurance premiums, property taxes, depreciation of the property, and maintenance expenses from your total taxable income.

Network

You can join an organization or forum that will help you reach out to other landlords and rental property investors. It not only helps with networking, but you will be surprised by all that you can learn by talking to others. Sharing ideas and advice will help you grow and become a better owner.

Self-managing the property certainly requires a commitment and is a responsibility you cannot afford to overlook if you want to be profitable. So, keep the steps discussed in this chapter in mind while self-managing the property.

Chapter 7: Financing

Options

A lot of people are usually surprised by the economics of the turnover between rental properties and stock returns. How can a rental property do better than conventional stocks while having a lower level of volatility and risk? Doesn't a high turnover usually imply greater risks? The answer is quite simple: unlike trading in stocks, the entry barrier to investing in rental properties is higher. Anyone can start investing in the stock market with capital as low as $100. It is one of the significant advantages of investing in the stock market, regardless of its volatility. However, when it comes to investing in rental properties, the returns are high, and the risk is comparatively low. There are two challenges a potential rental property investor must face, and they are the high capital required to acquire the property and the skills necessary to manage the investment successfully. Up until now, you were provided with information about how to select a property and analyze it; in this section, you will learn about the financing options available to you.

A down payment on the rental property is a significant expense you will incur. However, there are certain financing options you can use without having to worry about a down payment. These options are as follows.

House Hacking

The simplest and perhaps the easiest way in which you can buy a rental property is house hacking. A significant advantage of this option is that you can pay for the property while living in it for free. The concept is rather simple: you buy a multifamily unit and occupy one of the units while you rent the other units. The rent you get from the other units will help pay for the mortgage and other housing expenses, while you get a place to reside. Also, when you finally move out, the property will still function as a rental unit, and your cash flow will increase.

Are you wondering how this will help with the down payment? A mortgage lender will charge a much lower down payment on a property that's occupied by the owner when compared to other investment options. It is based on a simple risk calculation - the chances of a borrower defaulting on a loan on their own home is lower than the chances of default on a loan needed for rental property. A very popular loan option with an extremely low rate of a down payment is the FHA (Federal Housing Association) loan that requires a down payment of only 3.5%, provided your credit score is more than 580. If your credit score is less than 580, then I suggest you work on paying off the existing debts before you think about investing in a rental property.

FHA is not the only option available, and in fact, there are certain loan schemes which require a smaller down payment, or even no down payment altogether. So, you must inquire about the different mortgage schemes provided by at least three different local lenders before you choose your financing option.

Seller Financing

Wait a moment - who says that you need to opt for a loan to finance the rental property investment? At times, the sellers offer to finance the property for you, and you can negotiate terms with the property's seller. This means you can negotiate a deal sans any down payment. This is a good option when the seller has no mortgage or when the property was passed onto the seller as an inheritance. Maybe the property might need certain repairs, and the seller doesn't have the funds to pay for them. Often, such sellers are more than happy to accept regular monthly payments for the property and earn the income while quickly settling the property without having to deal with realtors and paying for their commissions. All sellers might not provide this option, but many will, provided you ask them about it. This is certainly an option you must not overlook, especially if you want to purchase a rental property without incurring any down payment.

Assuming the Seller's Mortgage

At times, the seller might not be ready to finance the rental property directly, but you can still acquire it without having to pay much or anything as a down payment. If the seller has an existing mortgage on the property, then you can offer to assume the same and make the mortgage payments. You will essentially be assuming the responsibility of paying off the existing loan. When you do this, you merely need to finance the remainder of the difference instead of worrying about making a hefty down payment.

Whenever you purchase a rental property using conventional financing options, the lender will not allow you to borrow unless you make a down payment. They do this to ensure that you are involved in the game and will make the rest of the payment without any failure. When you purchase a property by assuming an existing mortgage, you will have to make the mortgage payments and pay the seller any difference amount between the actual price of the property and previous mortgage payments made by the seller. You can pay the seller any way you want, such as borrowing the sum from your family or friends or even by using your credit card. You can also try to negotiate a loan with the seller.

Negotiating a Second Mortgage

You could find a lender who is willing to lend you funds equivalent to about 90% of the rental property purchase price. However, if you don't have the rest of the funds, then you can turn to the seller. All lenders don't offer this option, so before you go ahead and negotiate about the seller taking a second mortgage, you must clear terms with the primary lender. If you are opting for an FHA loan, then the option of a seller-held second mortgage is not available.

Collateral-Based Lending

Most of the conventional lenders, as well as FHA lenders, tend to be sticklers for rules. They might not allow you to borrow money from the property's seller or anyone else to allow you to finance the rental property without any down payment. However, every lender is not necessarily this fussy when it comes to the source of the down payment. Landlord lenders, as well as hard moneylenders, tend to lend funds based on the property as collateral instead of the borrower. The advantage of this option is that they aren't concerned with the source of the down payment, as long as it is not them. On the downside, they tend to offer a low loan-to-value ratio; this means the down payment required to be made will be higher. You must opt for a hard money lender for loans regarding any short-term renovations instead of a long-term loan. If you are investing in a property which can be rented out immediately, then you must look for an affordable long-term borrowing option. When you decide to opt for collateral-based lending from the landlord lender, then you can source the down payment from any other source of your choice like friends, family, the seller, personal loans, or any other source you can think of.

Another benefit of a landlord loan or any other collateral-based lender is that you will not be charged mortgage insurance. It essentially means that even when the interest rate payable is slightly higher, the monthly payments you make will be relatively lower since you don't have to pay for mortgage insurance.

Partners

As I have already mentioned, you can borrow from your family or friends for financing the property. However, who says you must restrict them to the role of money lender only? You can always take them on board as your investment partner. For instance, let us assume that you don't have the funds for a down payment, but you want to learn about investing in rental properties. On the other hand, your friend has the necessary funds but doesn't want to spend any time learning the tricks of the trade. Well, this couldn't have been more perfect. If your friend agrees to become a partner for the rental property investment venture, then they can provide the equity while you take care of the operations. This is a great way for your partner to earn passive income and for you to gain an investment opportunity.

Credit Cards

As with friends and family members, I have mentioned that you can pay using your credit card a couple of times to this point. Using a credit card to meet your financial requirements can be a good idea, since the line of credit is easily available. However, you must understand that most credit cards usually charge a cash advance fee that's anywhere between 3 to 4%, and the interest rate charged by them is quite high, too (around 10 to 25%). On the plus side, this is quite a flexible option, and you can use reward points to mitigate the cash advance fees. For instance, if you need $100,000 to purchase a rental property investment and the landlord is willing to lend you $80,000, you still need to come up with the remaining $20,000. You can use a cash advance from your credit card to finance this $20,000 requirement quickly. The one thing you must concentrate on is paying off the borrowed sum on the credit card as quickly as possible. Remember that the interest rates are quite high and the more you delay it, the greater will be the sum repayable. You are in a race against the clock now. If you think you can repay the borrowed sum within a couple of months, then this is an option you can consider. However, if you think that it will take you a couple of years to repay the borrowed sum, then steer clear of credit card debt.

HELOCs

Another wonderful idea for financing a rental property investment without any down payment is to borrow against your existing residence. HELOCs, or Home Equity Lines of Credit, will serve this purpose. You can gain a credit line against your current residence, and you can draw on it as the need arises. The rental income you earn from the property can be used for paying off the HELOC. Let me continue with the above-mentioned example. If you are borrowing $80,000 from the landlord, then you must secure the remainder of $20,000 to secure the rental property. It is cheaper to opt for HELOC instead of turning to credit cards, at least in terms of the interest rates chargeable. The up-front costs for starting a HELOC will be higher since the lender needs to run a title history on your current property and will charge you some junk fees. A HELOC is like a gift that keeps on giving. You can put it in rotation to buy rental properties, pull money out of it, repay it, and then repeat this process.

There are several reasons why you want to get a HELOC (equity line of credit), for example, to renovate a house, improve a home, or even invest in real estate. Installing a HELOC is not expensive and costs a fraction of the amount you are looking for. You may not need the money immediately. Nevertheless, it is very convenient if there is an excellent investment opportunity coming your way.

The qualifications you need to get a HELOC are very similar to those you need to meet to get a regular mortgage. The bank would require you to have a good credit rating and a good income, which can help you secure the amount for which you are applying. The requirements for all this vary from bank to bank, as well as your credit requirements. You must own the property that you are borrowing against. Capital is the difference between the value of your property and what you owe in relation to that property. Banks have different loan rates and costs. It also depends on the type of property you own (be it an investment or a personal residence).

The variable credit line for private homes is about 2% above that of Wall Street Prime, the minimum rate is 5%, and the maximum rate is 21%. You do not pay monthly or yearly fees, and you only have to pay interest on the money you use from HELOC. The bank must rate the property, and once this is done, the HELOC will be provided after paying multiple fees. With this form of a loan, you have the opportunity to repay the debt anytime that's convenient for you.

Other Options

The easiest way to use less money to buy rentals is to have a cheaper selection of homes. Market prices primarily determine the price of a rental property. You do not have to spend all your money on renting a property. You can buy something for a lower price and then decorate it if you want. You can also purchase rental properties as a renter. This means you can stay in this property for about a year and then rent it out. This technique saves you a lot of money. However, the payments you make for interest on loans and mortgages are higher. Higher fees usually hinder the flow of money from these investments.

Buying real estate for multiple families is another self-serving strategy. If you manage to buy a property that consists of about four parts, you can get a bank sanction to get a loan to a tenant if you live in it. If you wish, you can rent this unit after one year.

You can also reduce the amount of cash you need to buy a rental property by choosing Vendor Financing. One of the problems with financing the seller is finding a seller who is willing to provide you with the necessary credit. The cost of financing from the seller may be higher than your regular bank loan.

Another option is to work with another investor. This means that the amount you invest will be significantly reduced and you will continue to be able to share profits and make decisions. However, make sure that you have an agreement so that there are no unnecessary disputes in the future. An extremely risky strategy is to buy rented property by taking a hard cash loan and then refinancing that property into a traditional mortgage. Of course, to implement this strategy, you need a lot of experience, and it is quite risky.

The easiest way to save money on an investment is to save some of your income directly. You can save up to 50% of your investment income. It's not easy at all, no matter how much you make every month. Both our society and the economy are designed to make it easy to spend and hard to save. If you manage to control your spending habits, you can save more money. This does not mean that you should not spend money or live modestly. It means you have to spend your money wisely.

Saving your tax returns

You can save your tax refunds at any time for future investment. It is not difficult. You can set up your bank account so that when you receive a tax refund check, it will be credited directly to your savings account. That way, you'll make sure that you have not spent that amount on unnecessary things.

Set aside part of your payroll for investment

You can talk to your employer and get them to set aside part of your monthly salary for investment. If you are self-employed, you can instruct your bank to allocate part of your monthly income to real estate investments. You have to keep a certain percentage of your monthly income to live, of course. Depending on your comfort level, you can vary this percentage. It can be as high or as low as you like.

Living modestly

If you want to invest in the real estate market, you will undoubtedly need a lot of money. You can do this by living modestly for a while. Living modestly does not mean accepting a Spartan existence. For a while, you can prioritize your spending. You can set aside all expenses that seem superfluous or wasteful. You might desperately want to buy a pair of Louis Vuitton pumps, but this desire can certainly be suspended for some time. You'll be surprised at how much money you can save by prioritizing your spending. Anything that is not necessary can be delayed.

Additional sources of income

You can start your own business. If you have your own business, you have full control, and the opportunities to make more money are also high. Owning and maintaining rental properties can also be a business. You need to make sure you run the business, and not the other way around. A company should be able to make money for you without much effort.

An easiest way to get more money while you're part of someone else's business is to ask them. If you work for someone and know you are doing well, you can directly ask for a promotion. If you think you have no reason to ask for a pay raise, work harder so you can ask for what you deserve. If you think that you have reached a saturation point in your current job, you may want to consider making a career change. You can turn to what you like and like to do. It is never too late to do what you enjoy and are passionate about. There are different ways that you can make more money by doing what you want, and many of your passions can be turned into hobbies that earn you side income.With this income, you can invest in real estate.

Chapter 8: Exit Strategies

Investing in rental properties is an excellent way to develop a stream of passive income and increase your cash flow, but it is not always easy. It is quintessential that while purchasing a rental property, you develop an exit strategy, too. You never know when you might have to quit the game and to help you do this, you require an exit strategy. Most investors don't pay any heed to this and tend to suffer a loss when they try to get out of the game. It is a good idea to think about how you might need to exit the rental property market and consider this while investing.

You might want to invest in multiple rental properties to substitute your income or add on to your current income. The end goal might be to generate passive income, which gives you the financial freedom to pursue your dreams and maybe even quit your day job. It all sounds quite wonderful, doesn't it? That said, you might wonder why you will need an exit strategy when you like the steady rental income. Well, there might be some reasons or situations which will prompt you to sell the property, and when that does happen, you need an exit strategy.

Here are a couple of reasons why you might want to sell the property:

You might have had some bad experience, like dealing with horrible renters, poor property management and the like. I am certain a lot of people tend to sell their rental properties because of this reason. You need to understand that dealing with a bad renter is a very real possibility and it is just a part of being a rental property owner. A bad tenant can cost you a lot of resources - time as well as money. Appointing a bad property management team can also worsen the situation further and is at times the cause of all the trouble you are facing. It is not easy to find the perfect property management team, and the inability to do this can cost you dearly (if you don't want to self-manage the property). A good property manager makes all the difference in being successful or unsuccessful. I suggest that if you ever come across any such problem, the best thing you can do is fire the property manager or property management team and hope that things will turn around for you.

You might face a personal emergency. Life is full of uncertainties, and misfortune can befall anyone at an inopportune moment. If you are experiencing a personal emergency or a financial crisis, then it might be time to let go of the rental property. This is quite understandable. At times like this, you must concentrate on minimizing the losses by using a good exit strategy. You will learn more about this in the following sections.

Maybe you were looking forward to being a rental property investor, but as time went by, you realized that being a landlord is not meant for you. You might have tried and concluded that you need to quit being one. This does happen, especially when a new landowner tends to take on more than they can handle and manage. If you ever reach this point, I suggest that you give rental property investing another chance and hire a good property manager. Yes, it will eat into your profits, but at least it will help trigger the cash flow.

You might be interested in making a move on to better and bigger investments. This might be the only positive reason why you might want to sell an existing rental property. If you think you are headed toward bigger investments, then you will need to mobilize your finances for the same. If you are at this stage, then don't feel bad about letting go of one investment and instead think of this as progress.

Types of Exit Strategies

Since there are several reasons why you might need to exit from the rental property investment business, it is certainly wise to have an exit strategy in mind while purchasing the property. At times, things might seem peachy on paper, but the reality might be quite different. To quote Mike Tyson, "Everyone has a plan until they get punched in the face." You might have certain ideas about how the property needs to perform, but you certainly need to have at least one good exit strategy in mind before you even purchase the property. You can change the exit strategy over time, but at least you will be prepared when things don't go as expected. Markets can fluctuate, your fiscal position might change, or even your terms of the loan. A smart investor always has an exit strategy. Here are a couple of good rental property exit strategies you can consider.

Sell

Most rental property owners concentrate solely on the monthly rental income. They tend to spend so many hours crunching numbers and figuring out the monthly ROI that they forget to think about the big picture. It is quite rare that a rental property owner will hold onto the property forever unless it is in a perfect location and the returns from the property will never diminish. The chances of selling the property are quite high. So, the question isn't why you would want to sell, but when you will sell. Are you looking to hold onto the property for a specific period until you can recover your investment? Is there a number at which you might be willing to sell the property at any moment? These questions might seem like something you would consider a couple of years down the road, but you need to answer them right now. Any repairs or any improvements/ enhancements you do will affect the future value of the property. The decisions you make now will determine the property's value a couple of years later. If you are aware of when and why you want to sell the property, it will enable you to make better decisions in the present.

Own outright

The idea of being able to own the property outright and netting all the rent you receive is quite tempting. However, unless you are willing to part with a rather significant amount as down payment, this will take at least a couple of years to occur. Your plan to pay down or repay the loan must begin with the first payment. You must consider your repayment schedule if you want to be able to own the house outright and as quickly as you possibly can. The more you contribute toward the principle, the easier it will be to repay the remainder of the loan. This strategy will work regardless of whether you opted for a 15 or a 20-year loan. It certainly cannot happen overnight, but think about not having to worry about any repayments. You can use the rental property as a means to secure your retirement. The expenses you will need to pay for will be the property tax, insurance, and any other utilities. If this is your ultimate objective, then you will need to start working effectively toward it from the get-go.

Refinancing

There are a couple of other options available that many rental property owners are unaware of. Rental property loans and schemes have certainly had quite a makeover in recent times. That said, if you have the required credit score and equity, the number of options available to you increases. One option you can use as an exit strategy is refinancing. Loans meant for this purpose tend to have a ceiling rate of 75 to 85% of the loan value, and it depends on the number of rental units. This means the new loan can extend to up to 7% of the appraised value. You must pay off the existing primary lien and hold onto any excess cash to use for any other purpose. If you use it properly, then you can use it to expand your business or even collect it for a future down payment. Either way, if you have the necessary equity but aren't interested in selling the property, then you should consider refinancing.

HELOC

If you want to hold onto the property, then you can add a new home equity line of credit or HELOC. A HELOC functions like a second mortgage in addition to the existing lien. Everything related to the initial loan stays the same, but now you have another loan backing it. HELOCs are unique in terms of the repayment they offer, the rates, and the fees applicable. A HELOC provides the option of only having to repay the interest for the first ten years followed by the repayment of capital for the next ten years. This helps ensure your costs stay as low as possible.

Staying put

At times, the best thing to do is to do nothing. This might sound rather contradictory, but you can hold onto the property even without a specific exit strategy. Now, if push comes to shove, you must be able to act. However, you can give yourself a specific timeframe to evaluate your position. You can evaluate your positioning after a year, at the end of five years, or even ten years. What you must not do is keep making the mortgage payments without having a specific end goal in mind. Take some time and decide what you want to do with the property.

The absence of an exit strategy will prevent you from making sound decisions based on reason and thought. By preparing yourself for the unexpected, you can ensure that you are always a step ahead and nothing catches you unawares.

Chapter 9: Stages of a Screening Process

There are five stages of a screening process, and they are as follows.

- The first contact - This is the step wherein the prospective renter calls you to inquire more about the property or the lease. You must ask some pre-screening questions at this stage to ensure the prospective renter is a genuine one and isn't wasting your time.

- The showing - Once the prospective renter clears the first stage, the second stage is to show the rental property to the renter. This will probably be the first time you are meeting the renter, and you must look for certain red flags at this stage.

- The application - If the prospective renter is happy with the property and you are still interested in renting the property, then the third phase sets in. It is now time to get the renter to fill out an application that includes references from any past landlords as well as the current employers. You must run a credit and a criminal check on the renter.

- Approval process - If the tenant seems to tick off all the right boxes, then you must accept such tenants and decline the offers of the other applicants. Until the moment you sign the rental agreement, the screening process goes on.

- Signing the contract - Once you and your prospective renters are both happy with each other and the property, it is time to make things official. You must sign the rental agreement and carefully go through all the points included in it. You must also ensure that you and the renter agree on all the terms and conditions mentioned in the lease.

These are the five steps of a screening process, and you will learn about them in greater detail in this section.

First Contact

An experienced landlord is aware that nothing can be more troublesome than having to deal with a bad tenant. Essentially, most of the problems a landlord faces due to his or her renters can be avoided by following an effective screening process. If you don't implement certain consistent steps while screening the tenants, then you must start following all the tips given in this chapter.

When to start screening?

The screening process doesn't commence after receiving the rental application or before signing the rental application. In fact, for most rental property owners, it is a good idea to start thinking about screening the tenants from the first contact before showing the property to the prospective renter. The point of the first contact is when the prospective renters approach you through call or email to let you to know that they are interested in the property. There are certain pre-qualifying questions you can ask the interested parties to screen out the bad tenants. You must establish a simple dialogue before meeting the tenant by asking certain questions, which will help gauge the seriousness of the tenant about renting the property.

Questions to include

The first question you need to ask is, "Why do you want to move?" This question might seem like it doesn't concern you, but it does. I suggest you carefully note the answer you receive, because a prospective renter might at times want to move out because he or she is being evicted or due to a poor relationship with the previous landlord. If the prospective renter seems to complain about the existing landlord or their living situation, it is often because they are bad tenants (but not always - there are bad landlords out there, too). Look for prospective tenants who have some legitimate reasons for moving, like needing a bigger residential property or because they are changing jobs and such.

The second question you must ask the renters is, "When are you planning to move in?" If the tenant readily responds with a vague "Maybe tomorrow or even next week", it might mean the tenant isn't that good of a planner. Responsible tenants will start their search for a rental property months in advance in a planned manner. Most landlords usually need a 30-day notice period before a tenant moves out. If you feel that the timing will not work for you, then you don't have to show the property to the renter.

The third question you ask must be related to the monthly income of the potential tenants. The basic idea is to find renters who earn about 2.5 to 3 times the rent payable. This is just simple math, which will help figure out whether the prospective tenants will be able to pay the rent promptly. Once you inquire about this, the next question you must ask them is whether they will have the security deposit along with the first month's rent ready upon signing the rental agreement. This will help evaluate the renter's financial health. Steer clear of those tenants who offer to pay the security deposit in installments.

The next question you must ask is related to obtaining any references from their previous landlords and employers. If the potential renters cannot provide the necessary references or keep making excuses, then don't hold your breath unless the potential renter is just shifting from their parent's home for the first time. Once you receive the references, you need to do your due diligence. Also, while asking for references, ensure that you are asking for a former landlord instead of an existing one.

The final question you must ask is about whether the potential renters will be willing to provide a rental application and give their consent for a credit/background check or not. The answer to this question must be either yes or no. Any candidate who says no must be immediately disqualified. If someone doesn't want to comply with a credit or background check, it is usually because they have a spotty record. You must not ignore such instances.

There is one bonus question you can pose, and that's related to the number of people who will be living in the rental property. You might have to adjust the rent, the security deposit, or even restrict the number of people who can reside in the property. Most states have laws which say that a valid lease cannot allow more than two people per bedroom.

If you plan on asking these questions over a phone call, then quickly jot down the answers you receive and compare them with what the potential renter included in the rental application. If you notice any differences and discrepancies in answers received from this stage and the one where the rental application is submitted, it is an obvious red flag. Also, there are certain things you must keep in mind while dealing with the replies you receive from the renters.

- You must not make up your mind during this interview unless it is about paying heed to certain red flags.

- You don't have to make any exceptions because the potential renter is telling you a sob story.

- You must never make a decision based on such sob stories.

- You must always ask them for a credit report; you cannot overlook this step.

Show the Property

Once you are happy with the answers of the prospective tenants in the previous step, it is time to move on to the next step. The second step of the screening process is to show the property to the potential renters. While you are showing the property to them, it gives you a chance to evaluate things for yourself quickly. Also, you will learn about certain red flags you must pay attention to in this section.

Tips to follow

While showing the property, your main aim must be to get the prospective tenant to convert into a definite tenant. You must make the tenant want to rent your property. Not just that, you must also concentrate on finding good tenants. Here are certain tips you can use while showing the property:

You must consider the property's curb appeal. It means you must ensure the hedge around the curb is well maintained and trash is not lying around. Debris and overgrown hedges will make a prospective tenant wary about renting the property. The first impression of the property does matter. If you are aware of any existing problems in the property, then please get them fixed before you show the property to the renters. You must take care of any leaky faucets, paint that's peeling off, a pest infestation or any other problems that the renter might notice. When a potential renter sees a messy property, that person might conclude that it is okay to mistreat the property since the owner isn't interested in taking care of it.

You need to have certain selling points about the property on hand that you can discuss. Talk about the large bedrooms, the amenities offered, storage space, and any other features you can think of. You might not have considered yourself to be a salesperson up until now, but you are certainly trying to sell the property here.

Please turn on the lights and ensure that the prospective tenant can view the property in the best lighting. Apart from this, you need to regulate the temperature to make it pleasant and comfortable. You might also want to prepare yourself by carrying a rental application, authorization forms for background and credit check, and so on.

Red flags to watch out for

You might have often heard that it is unfair to judge a book by its cover. However, in this case, please judge away. This will probably be the first time you have met the prospective renter personally. You can learn about the prospective renters based on how they carry themselves, the observations they make, and the way they respond to you. I know it might sound rather shallow, but this is quintessential since it concerns your ability to earn returns from your investment. The first thing you can do is to pay attention to their choice of vehicle. Does the vehicle look well maintained, or does it look like a mobile dumpster? It is quite likely that the potential renter will treat the property the same way the car is being treated.

You can also observe the family dynamic and meet any others who might be moving in with the tenant. You can also make a note of their manners. Did the tenants wipe their feet before entering, do any of them smoke, and so on? Make a mental note of the positive as well as negative traits you observe. Apart from this, there are certain red flags you must watch out for.

Did more people show up to view the property than the renter had implied or mentioned during the phone call or the email? Please make sure you are aware of who you will be renting the property to. Each renter needs to submit an application and also give you the necessary authorization to conduct a credit and a background check. You must not allow those who are not a party to a rental agreement to live on the property.

Did your prospective renter speak ill about the existing or previous landlords? What are the complaints you kept hearing about? Will you be able to validate such complaints by checking their references? The usual reasons why a landlord-renter relationship turns sour are money and behavioral troubles. These are two things you must not inherit from the renter. Does the new renter seem to be in a hurry to find a property? Unless the tenant has a good reason to justify the rush,

103

it is often a sign of some trouble like an eviction from their current housing.

Did the new tenants turn up on time, or were they quite late? You can use the answer to this question to gauge whether they will be punctual about their monthly rents or not. Was it easy to coordinate with the prospective renters? An ideal situation is one wherein your renter will pay the rent on time and take good care of the property. However, this doesn't happen quite often, and you will need to coordinate with the tenant. You must ensure that the tenant will be able to take good care of the property.

Did you catch your tenants criticizing the property? If they aren't yet renting the property and have already started to complain, it is a red flag you must spot immediately. If the potential tenants are like this before the tenancy, then it will only get worse when they are the actual tenants. Carefully listen to all the questions your new tenants might ask. The questions they ask will help you understand the things that do and don't matter to them. It helps you understand how they prioritize things in relation to the property.

Rental Applications

In this section, you will learn about the essential aspect of the screening process - the rental application. The different topics covered in this section include what must be included in the rental application, who needs to fill it out, and how you can use the information provided by the tenants to make up your mind.

So, who all needs to fill out the rental application? The answer is quite simple - all those who are interested in renting the property need to fill out a form. Apart from this, all those individuals who will be living on the property or are paying a portion of the rent for the property (as is the case with parents paying the rent for their children to stay) must complete the application process. Whenever someone expresses their interest in your property, your prompt reply must be "I need all prospective renters or individuals who are paying a portion of the rent to complete a rental application and even authorize a credit/ background check. So, do you agree to this?"

When you do this, it shows that the rental application process isn't discriminatory, and you are treating all prospective tenants in the same manner. From a business standpoint, it allows the candidates to either select or reject their candidacy for the rental property.

Are you wondering what self-select and self-reject mean? There are two kinds of tenants you will not want to deal with, and you can easily allow them to filter themselves out from the screening process. The first kind consists of such individuals who might be good tenants, but they are not ready to commit to becoming a tenant yet. For instance, if the tenant is just getting started with the process of searching for properties, it is unlikely that the tenant has an answer readily available. Such tenants will need some time to shop around the market, look at different properties, compare the benefits and drawbacks of the properties, and analyze the same before making a decision. They might make good tenants, but dealing with such tenants is usually a futile endeavor. Instead, you can let them know that if they are interested in the property, they need to pay an application fee, and this will weed out such tenants.

The second kind of tenants are the one you don't want to deal with and are bad tenants. The bad tenants tend to filter themselves out of the application process, and you don't have to lift a finger. The rental application you provide the prospective tenants will require all the applicants to fill in all the details. By doing this, the tenants who have a bad credit score or have a history of causing trouble will not want to complete the application process let alone pay the application fee. So, you get to screen the tenants without doing much work. Design the questions such that the tenants will self-accept or self-reject.

Accept and Reject

In this section, you will learn about how to make a decision as far as accepting or rejecting an applicant as well as the traits that make a good renter so that you know when you have made a good decision. You will also learn about the best way in which you can reject an applicant.

There are certain things you can look out for to ensure that you are landing a good tenant at the end of the screening process. The first thing you must understand is that the rental application by itself will not tell you whether a candidate can be a good or a bad tenant. You will need to do some research to reach that answer. By now, I am sure you will have called the previous landlords and employers to learn more about the potential tenant. The employer might have confirmed the tenant's employment, and the conversation with the landlord must not have given rise to any red flags. If you have yet to make these calls, then I suggest you do that immediately. Here are certain things you must look for while searching for a good tenant:

The first thing a good tenant offers is stability. If you have done your due diligence, then you might be wondering what the positive attributes are that you can check for to confirm if the candidate will be a good tenant or not. You need to assess the stability of the tenant. You can do this by checking their duration of employment with the existing employer. Usually, an employee who has been working at a specific place for a couple of years is considered to be stable. If someone stays with an employer for two years or more, it is likely that such a person is looking to develop a long-term relationship with the employer. If the tenant has a stable and steady source of income, then you will receive the rent promptly.

You must check the disposable income of the tenant. It might seem like you are intruding, and it is none of your business. But in truth, it is your business, and you cannot overlook the tenant's earnings. By figuring out the tenant's disposable income, you can check whether such an individual can afford to pay the rent or not. A simple rule you can apply is the three-times rule. If the tenant's income is at least thrice the rent you are charging, then such an individual is a good tenant and will be able to pay the rent.

However, since you were checking the credit score, you can go a step ahead. The three-times rule doesn't consider the other expenses the tenant needs to account for. This is the reason why it is important to run a credit check on the tenant and understand the existing monthly debt payments and see the way it affects the affordability rule. The best rule to follow is the 40% rule. The rule is quite simple, and it states that the rent payable must not be over 40% of the tenant's gross monthly income less all the other debt obligations for the month.

Credit report

Why do you need to obtain a credit report? A lot of landlords skip this step, and it costs them dearly later. Now is the time to use the help of a neutral third-party for performing a check to estimate whether the tenant has a good credit score or not. It essentially helps determine the creditworthiness of a candidate. A lot of landlords tend to skip this step because they don't think of the relationship as they should - as the tenant's creditor. The tenants who agree to move into the property will do so, and in exchange for this, they promise to make a series of payments stretched over a period. You have delivered your end of the bargain, and now you merely need to wait for the tenant to catch up. The tenant will keep paying the monthly dues until the time of renewal of the agreement. This certainly sounds like a relationship that exists between a debtor and a creditor. So, treating the landlord-tenant relationship any different doesn't make any sense.

By using a credit check, you can find out about the debt the tenant has and the reported income to determine whether the tenant can afford the property or not. The total reported income of the tenant minus the monthly debt payments gives you the tenant's disposable income. Does this still look as attractive as the tenant's reported income? You can also check their payment history to see if they are on time with their payments or not. If the tenant isn't usually on time with their payments, then ask yourself whether that is something you can deal with or not. Apart from this, the credit report will also help validate certain items on their rental application.

Sign the Rental Agreement

The last step of the screening process is to sign the rental agreement. In this section, you will learn about the rental agreement and the final chance you have to screen the tenant before handing over the property keys. You will learn about how you can use the process of signing the lease to remove any lingering doubts you have about the renter. You might be wondering what you can do if you have already approved the tenant. Well, it is never too late to tear up the lease and search for another applicant. However, you must do this before the tenant signs the documents.

Reviewing the rental agreement

You must take some time to review the rental agreement with the tenant. You can do this in person or even over the phone. Please start with the most important aspects of the lease like the rent payable, any late fees when rent isn't paid on time, the necessary security deposit, the terms of moving in and moving out, and the rules about the eviction process. If there are any utility fees, pet fees, or any other fees payable, then you must mention these to the tenant. After stating each term, ensure that you and the tenant are both in agreement.

Once you are done discussing the major terms of the contract, you must review all the subclauses mentioned in the document. You must be familiar with all the terms included in the contract, all of your rights, and you should also be able to answer any questions the tenant might have. Then, you must review all the rules and regulations about the lease. Let the tenant know about all the different penalties in place when any of the terms are violated.

When you do this, you give yourself one opportunity to spot a massive red flag - whether the tenant is serious about making this commitment or not. Is the tenant respectful while reviewing the contract? Is the tenant attentively listening to what is being discussed? If yes, then your tenant is quite serious about it. On the other hand, if the tenant seems the least interested in going over all these things, it shows the tenant isn't aware of the commitment or the financial obligation being made. The tenant screening process is not just important because it is a part of the due diligence you must undertake, but it also sets the stage for any future troubles.

Security deposit, first month's rent, and the move-in fees

It is a common practice for the tenant to pay the first month's rent while signing the rental agreement. Also, now is the time to ask the tenant to pay the security deposit along with any moving-in fees. If you are expecting such payments, then you must communicate the same to the tenant while reviewing the contract. The tenant must bring the necessary checks for payment, and you can deposit them after the rental agreement has been signed. To avoid any unnecessary confusion, I suggest you do all of this at least two weeks before the rental agreement kicks in. The first payments you receive are a measure of how the tenant will pay the monthly dues from now on.

The tenants must either carry the payments with them or must deposit them in your account within a couple of days of signing the contract. If the payments don't clear within three days to one week, or if you don't receive the payments within this duration, then don't let the tenants move in. By asking the new tenants to make all these payments, you are essentially gauging whether the tenant has the necessary finances to make the payments or not. Once the rental agreement has been signed, it is considered to be a voidable contract if the payments for the security deposit or the first month's rent don't clear. The tenants made a promise to pay, and since they defaulted on the payment, you can rescind the contract, and the rental agreement will be void henceforth. However, if you do allow them to move in and it is not an issue about whether the contractual obligations have been fulfilled, you can now resort to the tenancy laws and evict the tenant for the non-performance of their obligations.

Setting a deadline

If the tenant doesn't sign the rental agreement onsite when you meet, then ensure that you inform the tenant about the deadline for signing. At times, the tenants might feel pressured and will not want to sign the contract on site. This is quite normal, and you can give the tenant some time to sign the contract. The natural extension given for signing the lease is between 24 to 48 hours. Until the tenant has signed the contract and the payments have cleared, you must not take the property off the market. Also, inform the tenant about this policy.

If the tenant seems to think that the 24 to 48 hour allowance isn't much to review the agreement and sign it, that's a red flag you must watch out for. It means that the tenant is applying for other properties and hasn't decided about the property he or she wants to rent. If the tenant signs the rent agreement elsewhere, then it means it was all a waste of your time. So, whenever a tenant implies that 24 to 48 hours isn't sufficient time, then stick to your guns. You are running a business, and you need to set deadlines to show the tenant that you cannot hold the property waiting for their confirmation and that you too can pursue other applicants.

While going through all the rental applications, you must keep a couple of applicants as a backup. That backup list will certainly come in handy now.

Note: Please ensure that the rental agreement is in compliance with all the local, state, and federal laws that apply. You need to provide all the necessary disclosures in the document. Apart from this, you must also provide any receipts for the payments you receive, like the security deposit and such.

Chapter 10: Increase

Tenant Retention Rate

Do you want to increase your return on investment (ROI) from your rental property? If yes, then you must concentrate on reducing the turnover. Turnover refers to vacancy, the period wherein you are not earning any rents but are still repaying the mortgage or a property loan. It isn't merely restricted to the mortgage, but you will need to pay for the necessary maintenance expenses, too. When the property is vacant, and you are searching for prospective tenants, you will need to spend on marketing, advertising, hosting open houses, collecting and processing the rental applications you receive, scanning prospective tenants, and maybe even making calls to their employers or prior landlords for verification. If you employ a property manager, then you will need to continue to pay such an individual even when the property is vacant.

Put simply, turnovers can eat into your bottom line. So, the best way to rectify this is to ensure the property is not usually vacant. The trick is to hold onto your good tenants. In this section, you will learn about different tips you can use to increase your rate of tenant retention.

Understand the Market

You might have a great relationship with your tenants, but if the property is overpriced, doesn't have much connectivity or is outdated when compared to some other property in your area, then the tenants will look elsewhere. While searching for the ideal neighborhood, spend some time understanding the market, too. You must be aware of any real competition in the market along with the rents they are quoting and their reasons for it. Compare other properties to the one you own, and you will be able to get a rough idea of whether your property will fare well or not in comparison. You must step into the shoes of a tenant and think about the various factors that might appeal to them as well as any expectations they might have about the property.

Every couple of months, please go check any vacant rental properties available in your neighborhood. As soon as you enter the property, start thinking like a prospective tenant and make a list of all the different amenities that appeal to you. Apart from this, you can also attend other open houses. If you aren't sure what renters usually look for in properties, then why don't you try talking to a couple of potential renters? Ask them what they think about your property and the things they might want to change.

Also, if you have had any previous tenants, then you must conduct exit interviews, too. Ask them for their feedback about their tenancy, the things they liked, the changes they might want to make, and their reasons for moving out. All of this information will help you get the right read on the property.

List of Improvements

You must learn about all the different improvements a tenant might want to make to the property. This means you must not stop conducting exit interviews or talking with other prospects living in the neighborhood. The best source to understand what the renters want is to talk to them! You can also conduct a semi-annual inspection with the tenants and inquire about all the different changes they would love to make if it were possible. Essentially, you are asking the tenants about what their "dream" rental property is like. Make a note of all the changes they suggest and keep adding to it. You don't have to make all the changes, and be prepared to come across certain outlandish and even ridiculous suggestions. You can make all the changes that are affordable and will help increase the property's value. Make those changes that guarantee a good return on the money you invest.

Once you make such changes, your tenants will feel like they are heard, and their opinions are valued. This, in turn, can make them want to stay put instead of shifting from your property.

Referral Program

If you own several single-family units in a specific neighborhood or have a multifamily building, then here is a simple strategy you can use. Most people like the idea of living near their friends or family members. So, what could be better than being neighbors with the people they love? Announce to your tenants that if they refer the property to their friends or any of their family members, then you will give the friend a voucher to cover the expenses of moving. This is an important point; you must offer the incentive to the person they referred the property to and not the tenant. By doing this, you can easily fill up the vacancies, and your tenants will be happy to have their loved ones nearby.

Screening is Important

You must screen any potential renters before you decide to let out the property. This is one of the most important aspects of becoming a landlord or a property manager. It also has a direct effect on your total turnover. A bad tenant might need to be evicted, or at the very least, you might not want to renew the agreement with such a tenant. By signing a rental agreement with a bad tenant, you merely increase your turnover. It isn't restricted to tenants who don't pay their rent on time or even those who damage the property. You must also screen out any potential house hoppers - those tenants who frequently shift from one place to another. You must look for a stable tenant who will not only pay the rent on time, but will also take good care of the property. It is always a good idea to find a tenant who is willing to stay put for longer if you want to reduce the chances of the property being vacant.

Maintain Reference Files

It is a good idea to maintain reference files. Will you be able to remember important details about your tenants like their occupation, job profile, names of their children, their hobbies, and so on? It is impossible to remember a lot of details. So, create a small reference file for each of your tenants. Add a couple of notes in it about what they do, their birthdate, anniversary, or other important dates. Along with it, make a brief note of every interaction you have with the tenant. Whenever you talk to the renter, even if it is a brief conversation, by recollecting certain details about their lives, you can make the renters feel good.

For instance, it can be something as simple as "Hi, Mr. Smith. How are you doing? The last time we spoke, you told me that John was about to start at a new school. How does he like his new school?" It might sound like a silly thing to do, but by doing this, you can develop a better relationship with your tenant. Your tenants might even be pleasantly surprised that you remember details about their lives, and this ensures friendlier conversations.

Raise the Rent

There are different reasons to increase the rent on an annual basis, even if the hike is a small amount. It helps increase your revenue. Also, you don't want your rent to be lower than the market rate, do you? It helps to increase the rent in small increments instead of giving the tenants notice about a major rent hike.

Don't forget about setting your tenant's expectations - rents will increase every year. Your tenants must expect a slight increase in rents and be assured that they will not have to endure a massive increase in the rent payable. While setting their expectations, you can also offer certain conditions. Whenever the lease is up for renewal, here are three options you can give your tenants:

The first option- they can continue with the month-to-month rent basis with a marginal increase in the rent.

The second option- if they decide to renew the rental agreement for another year, then the rent hike will be less.

The third option is to offer them an option of renewing their rental agreement for the term of two years, where they can lock in that marginal rent hike for the second year.

If the tenants are aware of the fact that the rents will increase, then it will seem like a good idea to lock in a good rental price for the term of two years. This is what I meant by setting expectations.

Pick up the Phone and Call

If you know that a tenant's rental agreement is coming up for renewal, if the rent is late, or if you are filing for their eviction, then you must send a notice. Apart from this, please pick up the phone and call the tenant. According to the law, you must inform the tenant about certain things by sending notices, but it doesn't mean you must stop there.

It is a good idea to talk to the tenant over the phone before they receive formal communication, since the former helps elicit a decent conversation instead of sharp dialogue. If you want to maintain a good professional relationship with your tenants, then make that call and don't put it off. By doing this, you give the tenant a chance to explain their side of the story, too. It gives you a chance to understand why the tenant missed their rent bill. You can always file for eviction, but knowing the reason for it might change your mind. However, keep in mind that it is a business for you, so always be practical while making decisions.

Don't Barge into the Property

You must always call the tenant before you decide to enter the rental property. This applies to all properties regardless of the type of property. Yes, you must give written notice, but a phone call always helps. Even if it is an emergency, you are duty bound to inform the tenant about your intent before entering the premises. It is a simple way of showing that you respect the tenant's right to privacy. Sure, your property is your asset, and it is your business. To a tenant, the property is their home; learn to respect it. It hardly takes a couple of seconds to make a call like this, and it is a gesture your tenant will appreciate.

Prioritize the Responsiveness

Whenever there is a repair, then please attend to it immediately. If you delay fixing the repair, then the problem will merely fester and can also damage the property. Understand that it is urgent for your tenant, because any problem with their home will be an urgent one. Whenever your tenant reports any problem, ensure that you take action as soon as you can. Always keep a list of contractors handy according to their area of expertise and their costs. If there is any delay at all, please explain it to the tenant, too. When you do this, it shows the tenant that getting the problem fixed is your priority.

Sending Holiday Cards

Make it a point to send holiday greetings to your tenants, at least the "good" ones. If you are thoroughly screening the tenants, then this should include all of your tenants. Sending holiday cards is a good gesture, even more so if they are religion specific. If you know that your tenant celebrates a specific holiday, don't forget to send a holiday greeting. Address the greeting to each member of the tenant's family residing in your property. Try to make the greeting seem as personal as possible. It is not only a good gesture, but will certainly make the tenant feel valued.

Pruning is a Must

No, I am not talking about pruning the lawn. You need to prune your money tree - cut off any dead branches and pluck the rotten fruit. You can use your chosen plant metaphor for this analogy; you do understand where I am going with it, don't you? You need to get rid of bad tenants as soon as you can. Not only are they expensive, but any damage they do the property is an added expense for you. From fixing any damage to filing for eviction to pushing your good tenants to move, you cannot afford to hold onto any bad tenants if you don't want to hurt your bottom-line.

Regardless of how well you have implemented the previous tips, a good tenant will not stick around if their neighbors are troublesome. Each month, look at the rental agreements that are coming up for renewal. If you have your doubts about a specific tenant, send a non-renewal notice as soon as you can. If you have any doubts about holding onto a specific tenant, you already have the answer - you don't. You don't need to look for an explanation or a justification to keep a bad tenant because you don't want to meddle with your turnover. Remember that letting such a tenant stay will do you more harm than good in the long run. If you have good tenants, then it will certainly reduce your maintenance costs, too.

Chapter 11: Mistakes to Avoid

Making mistakes is part of the learning process. However, it is better to learn from the mistakes of others instead of making them yourself. Some mistakes can prove to be quite costly and might land you in hot water. To avoid all this, you must be aware of the common mistakes rental property owners make and how you can fix them. In this chapter, you will learn about such common mistakes along with the ways to avoid making them.

Mistakes to Avoid while Buying a Rental Property

Saving money and investing money tend to be necessary activities for an average individual. By doing this, you can create a financial safety net to fall back on in times of trouble. While saving money, it is quintessential that you carefully consider where you want to park your funds. Essentially, any form of investment you opt for must help you achieve your long-term financial goals. So, it is important you carefully select your stream of investment to grow your capital and increase your income while minimizing the risks involved.

Buying a rental property is one of the best forms of investment. Rental property investment has several advantages and usually offers a rather stable source of income when maintained properly. However, there are a couple of mistakes investors make while purchasing rental property. Here are the mistakes you must avoid making while purchasing a real estate investment property.

Concentrating only on appreciation

New investors tend to make the mistake of investing in a rental property solely based on its appreciation value. Please don't do this. The value of rental properties can fluctuate due to a variety of reasons, and if the market trends don't move like you hoped they would, then you stand the risk of incurring a huge loss. It is a good idea to consider the appreciation value of a property before investing, but it must not be the only criterion for investing. You might have to sell your property unexpectedly, and if the market conditions are not favorable, then you will only incur a loss. Instead, you must concentrate on the cash flow the property can generate. This is why you are required to thoroughly analyze the property and make all the estimates before purchasing. Also, ensure that you are obtaining all the historical data related to the property form the seller while investigating the property you want to buy.

A watertight contract

If you have any assumptions about the property you want to buy, ensure they are all included in writing in the purchase agreement. You must read the purchase agreement thoroughly to ensure it is watertight and no items are missing. While buying real estate, you will need to sign multiple contracts. It is likely that you might not understand all the terms related to it, so you can seek legal assistance for the same. Read the contract carefully, including the fine print, before you sign anything. Make sure all the important clauses and terms are present before signing. An item you overlooked or a missing item can prove to be a costly mistake. Don't hesitate to seek external help and hire a lawyer to help you throughout the process of signing the contract.

Hiring a third-party

Managing the rental property is quite important when you want to get into the business of rental property investing. The property must stay in good condition if you want to reduce your tenant turnover rate. It also helps attract potential tenants. Once you let it out, you must ensure it is being managed properly. Often, an owner might be required to immediately address any repairs or other problems related to the property, such as plumbing leaks, as quickly as possible.

If you ignore the problems, it can become an expensive expenditure. Working with in-house property management is a good idea so that the person selling the property is also responsible for the way the investment performs. You do have the option of hiring a third-party service like a property management agent, but it can prove to be quite costly and at times unreliable. The agency you employ might not be fully aware of all the different aspects of property management. Working with an in-house management company is a good idea. Please ensure that the company you decide to employ will be working even during the buying process. If you do have to hire a management company, ensure that you are overseeing their work and aren't leaving everything to them. You are the owner of the property, and any damage to it will eat into your earnings.

Lack of proper insurance

Insurance is quintessential while investing in rental properties. A lack of proper insurance makes your property vulnerable in case of adverse weather conditions like flooding or heavy snow. Failing to buy proper insurance or sufficient insurance is a rookie mistake you must avoid. Insurance needs to be carefully considered and understood while stepping into the world of rental property investing. Any insurance policy you opt for must be accepted only after taking into account different aspects like your financial situation and the location of the property. The insurance policy you purchase will help shield your property from any unforeseeable damage. Also, having the right coverage will indemnify your losses if you suffer any in the case of an unfortunate incident.

Too many properties

Since you are just getting started with rental property investing, it is a good idea to stick to only one investment at a time. Please do this until you get the hang of it. If you invest in too many properties at once, you will not only be spreading your finances quite thin, but you will also be unable to take proper care of all the properties. While getting started with rental property investing, test the waters before you jump into the deep end. Keep in mind that purchasing a home is quite different from investing in a rental property. It is a completely different ball game altogether. I suggest that a beginner must always start with one property, at least initially. By doing this, you will be able to get a fairly good idea of all that's involved. If possible, try to wait for 12 to 15 months before investing in another property. It gives you sufficient time to understand all the technicalities of managing a rental property. Once you decide that investing in rental properties is palatable to you, you can expand your investments. This will enable you to understand all the potential problems that can crop up. Think of the first investment you make as a learning experience to understand the business of rental property ownership.

Owning a rental property is certainly a great means to fulfill your financial dreams and generate passive income. By avoiding the mistakes discussed in this section, you can make the most of your investment.

Common Mistakes Rental Property Owners Make

There is so much more to managing a rental property that goes beyond collecting the rent due. If you are just getting started with owning and managing a rental property, then there are certain things you must be aware of. The most important of all is the fact that you must treat your rental property investment like you would treat a small business. The more knowledgeable you are about proper management, the smaller are your chances of making any costly mistakes. Owning a rental property can certainly be quite exciting, but it can be a difficult pill to swallow if you don't understand what you are doing. So, what are these common mistakes I am referring to? Read on to learn more about these mistakes and how you can avoid them.

Don't try to do everything by yourself

Owning a rental property is quite different from maintaining the property. Becoming a property owner is easy, but managing it can be a rather tricky process, especially if you don't do it properly. Usually, managing a property requires a lot of time, and it is an important responsibility you cannot overlook. The greater the number of tenants you must manage, the more difficult your work will be. Without the proper knowledge, skills, or experience, you might face some difficulties. At times the mistakes can prove to be costly and can land you in legal trouble, too. You can hire an in-house management company to help handle your first investment. While doing this, don't leave everything to them and instead learn the ropes. When you know what you are doing and how to do the job, you can start managing the property on your own. Don't try to do everything by yourself, and seek help when in trouble.

Only a specific service provider

If you do want to hire a property management agency, then you must be aware of the two types of companies - the ones which offer specific services, and the comprehensive service providers. For instance, you can hire a lease management company. It might seem like a good option cost wise, but it is not effective. A company like this will only handle the leases and will not pay much attention to finding good tenants for your property. After all the money you pay for their services, you will need to deal with the tenant whether they are good or bad. Dealing with a bad tenant can be quite stressful. On the other hand, if you hire the services of a management agency providing comprehensive services, then they will not only help you find good tenants but will help manage them, too.

Hiring a real estate agent

Every service provider has his areas of expertise. Even if veterinarians are doctors, it doesn't mean they're qualified to treat humans. Likewise, you must not hire a real estate agent to help you manage the property. Property management is quite different from dealing in real estate. Always approach professionals who provide the services you are looking for. Regardless of how wonderful the real estate agent is, the agent cannot provide you the kind of services a property manager can. Instead of wasting your hard-earned money on a real estate agent who has other priorities, you must hire someone who can get the job done for you. You must not only ensure that you are getting your money's worth, but that the property is well managed, too.

Charging the wrong rent

How you do you know whether you are charging the right rent or not? There are two ways to determine the answer - the first one is when you notice your turnover rates are quite high, you cannot fill the vacancy, and keep getting complaints about the rent being too high. The second method is when your income from the property is less than the income that properties similar to yours yield. Fixing the rent is not an impulsive decision, and you must spend considerable time doing the necessary research and analysis before deciding the rent. If you don't do this properly, then you will incur more losses and not see any profits.

Improper insurance

As mentioned in the previous section, it is quintessential to have the right insurance coverage for your property. Having natural calamity insurance will protect you from incurring any losses during a natural disaster. A lot of new investors don't understand the importance of proper insurance.

Clear rules

Renting a property is a contract you enter into with the tenant. As with any contract, you must set clear and unambiguous rules as well as terms and conditions. If you don't set any clear rules, it can become quite difficult to manage the tenants. The lack of proper rules can land you in unnecessary trouble. This is the reason why you must not only make a list of all rules applicable to the tenancy, but you must also allocate corresponding consequences if the tenant fails to comply. Once all the rules are in place and the tenant signs the rental agreement, both the parties involved are legally liable to follow the rules.

Unhealthy relationships

It is a good idea to have an amicable relationship with your tenants. However, you must also know where to draw the line. Being very friendly with the tenants can make them assume that they can take undue advantage of your friendship. Be friendly while being professional. In the end, you are in business. So, don't forget to treat it like one. If the tenants start to act irresponsibly, then they will only set a bad example for the other tenants.

Repairs and maintenance

A lot of property owners tend to pay for repair and maintenance work by themselves. It might seem like an ideal solution for you, but this is not a good idea in the long run. You might think it is unnecessary to seek outside or professional help with these issues. You must remember that even small maintenance and repair work, if not done properly, can lead to bigger troubles later. Poor resolution of issues can not only tarnish your reputation as a good property owner, but can even cost you your tenants. If there are any repair and maintenance issues, you must make sure you hire professionals who are competent enough to fix the issue. You own the rental property, and as an owner, the maintenance and upkeep of the property are responsibilities you cannot shrug away. Without the necessary experience, you might forget or fail to do certain things. So, don't try to do the job of a handyman if you have no experience in that field and instead hire help.

By avoiding the mistakes mentioned in this section, you can become a good rental property owner.

Legal Mistakes to Avoid

Being a landlord can be tricky at times, especially for newbies. Here are common legal mistakes landlords tend to make and the tips you can follow to avoid landing in any potential legal trouble.

Discriminating queries

The law prohibits a landlord from refusing to rent a property to a tenant based on the grounds of discrimination like the tenant's race, religion, nationality, sex, disability, familial status, and color. You must avoid asking the potential renters all such questions that seem discriminatory or suggest any intention of discrimination.

Failure to disclose

Different states have different requirements about the facts that must be disclosed. However, there are certain disclosures all landlords must make to their prospective renters. For instance, you must disclose to the tenant any mold that exists if you are aware of it or even have reason to believe that it exists. You must inform the tenants about any registered sex offenders living in the vicinity if you know the same. You must also disclose information related to any recent deaths that might have taken place in the rental property. According to Federal laws, the landlord must also disclose any details about the use of lead-based paints in case the property was constructed before 1978 in the US.

Illegal elements in the rental deed

A rental agreement must not contain any clauses or conditions that violate any laws of the state or any of the Federal provisions. You must avoid including any discriminatory or illegal conditions in the rental agreement like any provision that takes away the rights of the tenant to sue the landlord or the tenant's right to refund. The inclusion of any illegal terms can land you in trouble and make you liable to pay monetary damages.

Provide a safe environment

In most of the states, it is the landlord's legal responsibility to provide the tenants with a safe environment. As a landlord, you are liable to ensure that your tenants are safe from any potentially dangerous conditions on the property and are safe from any criminal activity. You must make the necessary inspections and inform the tenants or anyone else who enters the premises about any hazardous conditions that exist on the property. You must also take reasonable care to ensure the safety of your tenants from other tenants or any other criminals who enter the property. If the tenant sustains any physical harm or the property is damaged and the tenant was unaware of the unsafe environment, then the tenant has the right to sue the landlord. It is all about maintaining a full-disclosure policy when it comes to the property you want to rent.

Refusing to make repairs

While drafting the rental agreement, make sure that you specify the details of making repairs. You must make sure to spell out who this liability rests on. At times, you might have to make certain repairs even when the rental agreement doesn't cover such duties. Every state has laws about having an implied warranty regarding the habitability of the rental properties. A property is considered to be habitable if it provides heating, gas, clean water, is structurally safe (floors and roof), and has plumbing and electricity. If the property is in a state of disrepair, then the tenant has the option to make the necessary repairs and charge it to the owner's account, move out, or even report the apparent violations to a state building inspector. The failure to make the premises habitable is just a lawsuit waiting to happen.

Violating the tenant's right to privacy

The right to privacy is a universal fundamental right, and it applies to your tenants, too. A landlord must not enter a rental unit without giving the tenant a verbal or a written notice 24 hours before entering the premises. A landlord can only enter after giving the notice while repairing, showing the property to any prospective renters, or for the sake of inspecting. If it is an emergency, then this rule isn't applicable.

Eviction rules

As a landlord, you have the right to evict a tenant for not paying the rent, for violating any provision mentioned in the rental agreement, for the failure to vacate on the expiry of the lease, or if the tenant has caused some damage to the property which has led to the depreciation of the property's value. Before you can throw out the tenant, you must follow the due course of an eviction process. Every state has different guidelines about this topic, but a common requirement is that you must serve the tenant an eviction notice before you file a suit for eviction in the court of law. If you try to evict a tenant without following the due process, you are merely attracting a potential lawsuit wherein the tenant can claim compensatory damages.

Withholding the security deposits

Most rental contracts require the tenant to pay a security deposit for any potential damages caused by the tenant or due to the tenant's carelessness. Once a tenant moves out, you can use the amount of the security deposit to fix any damage thus caused. If you do this, then you are duty bound to provide the tenant with an enumerated list of all the necessary repairs and deductions you made and return any balance to the tenant. If you don't provide an itemized list of deductions or fail to return the remainder of the security deposit, you might be liable to pay monetary damages to the tenant.

Deal with abandoned property

If the tenant moves out but leaves certain items behind, then the landlord can treat it like abandoned property. The first thing you must do is notify the renter about claiming such property, the cost of storage if any, where to claim it from, how the property can be claimed, and the duration within which such claims must be made. If the property is unclaimed even after your due diligence, then you can sell the property after issuing a notice about it in the local newspaper if the property is worth more than a specific sum. If the property is below the state-specific limit, then you have the option of either retaining or discarding the property.

Inadequate insurance

Apart from insuring the property for any damage due to natural disasters, you must also insure it against any lawsuits initiated by the tenant. If you evict a tenant illegally, enter the property illegally, or if the tenant or any other person who is legally present on the premises is injured due to a hazardous condition, the insurance will help cover the costs of litigation or any legal action brought against you.

Keep these simple provisions in mind to prevent any legal trouble.

Conclusion

I want to thank you once again for purchasing this book. I hope it was an informative read.

You might be quite excited at the prospect of investing in rental properties now. One of the ideal investment choices you can make is to invest in a rental property. You might want to invest in rental properties for different reasons. Regardless of your reasons, investing in rental properties can be quite lucrative if you are diligent and invest carefully. Armed with all the information given in this book, you can now make informed decisions. You no longer have to seek other sources to learn about rental property investing. The information given in this comprehensive guide will help you get started with rental property investing.

So, all that's left for you to do is get started as soon as you want! While making any investment decision, please ensure that you carefully analyze the risks involved and the returns you can gain. Don't be in a hurry and do your due diligence. A little extra effort can indeed go a long way when it comes to investing. Once you successfully set up the rental property and lease it out, you can start earning passive income.

By following the simple steps and tips given in this book, you can attain the financial freedom you always dreamt of and wished for. The key to turning your life around is in your hands. So, act immediately and make the most of the resources available.

I want to thank you once again for choosing this book. If you found the information valuable and wish to let others know, please leave a review!

Reference

1st Steps to Rental Property Investment Analysis - Ideal REI. (2019). Retrieved from https://idealrei.com/how-to-analyze-rental-property

5 Mistakes To Avoid When Buying Rental Property - Cash Flow Connections. (2019). Retrieved from https://cashflowconnections.com/5-mistakes-to-avoid-when-buying-rental-property/

10 Steps To Successful Self Management. (2019). Retrieved from http://www.managemyproperty.com/blog/2016/06/10-steps-successful-management/

Carson, C. (2019). How to Pick the Ideal Location For Investment Properties - a Comprehensive Guide. Retrieved from https://www.coachcarson.com/ideal-location-investment-properties/

Common Landlord Mistakes and How to Avoid Them. (2019). Retrieved from https://www.c21propmgmt.com/landlord-mistakes/

Davis, G. (2019). How to Buy Your First Rental Property with No Money Down | SparkRental. Retrieved from https://sparkrental.com/how-to-buy-your-first-rental-property-no-money-down/

How to Find Rental Properties for Sale. (2019). Retrieved from https://www.thebalancesmb.com/find-rental-properties-for-sale-2124846

How To Start A Rental Property Business | FortuneBuilders. (2019). Retrieved from https://www.fortunebuilders.com/rental-property/

Jankelow, L. (2019). Screen Tenants Even When Signing the Lease | Avail. Retrieved from https://www.avail.co/education/articles/screen-tenants-even-when-signing-the-lease

Rental Property Exit Strategies | CT Homes. (2019). Retrieved from https://www.cthomesllc.com/2019/05/rental-property-exit-strategies/

Ten Landlord Legal Mistakes to Avoid - FindLaw. (2019). Retrieved from https://realestate.findlaw.com/landlord-tenant-law/ten-landlord-legal-mistakes-to-avoid.html

Top 5 Rental Property Exit Strategies. (2019). Retrieved from http://www.cashflowdiaries.com/top-5-rental-property-exit-strategies/

Turner, B., Turner, B., & Turner, B. (2019). The Five Success Principles of Rental Property Investing.